Dress Casually for Success ...
For Men

Mark Weber
and
The Van Heusen Creative Design Group

McGraw-Hill

New York   San Francisco   Washington, D.C.   Auckland   Bogotá
Caracas   Lisbon   London   Madrid   Mexico City   Milan
Montreal   New Delhi   San Juan   Singapore
Sydney   Tokyo   Toronto

Library of Congress Cataloging-in-Publication Data

Dress casually for success—for men / the Van Heusen Creative Design
   Group with Mark Weber.
     p.   cm.
  ISBN 0-07-001622-4
   1. Men's clothing. 2. Grooming for men. I. Weber, Mark, 1949-.
II. Van Heusen Creative Design Group.
TT618.D74 1996
646´.32—dc20   96-33532
                                             CIP

McGraw-Hill

*A Division of The **McGraw·Hill** Companies*

1 2 3 4 5 6 7 8 9 0 DOC/DOC 9 0 1 0 9 8 7 6

ISBN 0-07-001622-4

*The sponsoring editor for this book was Susan Barry, the editing supervisor was Fred Dahl,
and the production supervisor was Pamela Pelton. It was set in Palatino by Inkwell Publish-
ing Services.*

Printed and bound by R. R. Donnelley and Sons.

This publication is designed to provide accurate and authoritative information in regard to the subject matter covered. It is sold with the understanding that the pub-
lisher is not engaged in rendering legal, accounting, or other professional service. If
legal advice or other expert assistance is required, the services of a competent professional person should be sought.

*—From a declaration of principles jointly adopted by a committee of
the American Bar Association and a committee of publishers*

This book is printed on recycled, acid-free paper containing a minimum of
50% recycled, de-inked fiber.

McGraw-Hill books are available at special quantity discounts to use as premiums
and sales promotions, or for use in corporate training programs. For more information, please write to the Director of Special Sales, McGraw-Hill, 11 West 19th Street,
New York, NY 10011. Or contact your local bookstore.

Van Heusen, G. H. Bass, Gant, Izod, Izod Club are the registered marks of Phillips-
Van Heusen, Inc. and are used in this book pursuant to permission by Phillips-Van
Heusen, Inc. and may not be copied or otherwise reproduced without its express
written consent.

Photographer: David Sawyer
Stylist: Matthew Morris
Art Direction: Leslie Evans

Another book by Affinity Communications Corp.

Dress Casually for Success ... For Men

CONTENTS

FOREWORD

There are times when I reflect on other, more "noble" professions, in which individuals and teams are working on solving the world's problems, striving for global peace, eliminating disease, and educating our children. I ask myself how do we, in the apparel and retail professions, stack up next to those heroes? In truth, we don't and we can't.

Yet our industries play an important role in the greater good of humankind.

Clothing is one of the five essentials necessary to sustain life. We employ millions of people and provide for their families' well-being. While how you look should not matter in the greater scheme of life, it does. It matters to you and it affects how you feel about yourself and how others perceive you. While clothes do not "make the man," they can certainly help him to position himself for a more rewarding and comfortable day-to-day life and career. Our clothes, in the simplest terms, provide cover, warmth, and protection. Also, on a deeper level, clothes allow you to feel special and individualistic, allow you to stand out or blend in, while providing you with the ability to be comfortable in your head as well as with your body.

Phillips-Van Heusen has quietly built one of the largest apparel and footwear companies in the world. Our number 1 ranking in dress shirts, sweaters, and casual footwear will result in consumers spending over $3 billion on our products in 1996 worldwide. The strength of our corporation is in our brands: Van Heusen, G. H. Bass, Gant, Izod, Izod Club, and Geoffrey Beene. The strength of our brands comes from the people who have devoted their business lives to making those brands the right choice for millions of people around the world.

Our heroes are the 13,000 people of our corporation who labor throughout the United States and the world in developing and improving our products every day, every week, and every year. This book is dedicated to those 13,000 men and women who have brought us so far.

However, without the extraordinary efforts of a select few, this project would never have gotten off the ground. Those deserving of special appreciation are Bruce Klatsky, Chairman and CEO, our leader and my friend, in conjunc-

tion with Bruce Maggin, PVH Board Member who initiated and conceptualized the opportunity.

The Board of Directors of Van Heusen must be thanked for their support and direction that guides our growing corporation, as well as my fellow operating committee members: Allen Sirkin, Irv Winter, Michael Blitzer, and Manny Chirico, who are partners in the day-to-day managing of our corporation.

The incredibly talented Phillips-Van Heusen Design Team—Eileen Schwartz, Ezra Berkenwald, Michael Gorelick, Vicky Nordgren, Young Ju Hampton, Stephanie Wargo, Wes Walker, Read Worth, Judy Gordon, Laurie Hipple, Stephanie Cascarino, Sal Agati, Jeff Rose, Sarah Laurence, Jeff Bergus, Jeanne Clarke, Helen Katz, Michele Keating, Catherine Alessi, Nancy Hipple, Kelly Spatz, and Nica Larucci—helped develop what is in fact appropriate corporate casual clothing.

In particular, Mitchell Massey and Lynn Spindell of the Phillips-Van Heusen Marketing Department showed enthusiasm for the project that catapulted all of us to new heights, and Ken Wyse helped keep all of us on track with his extraordinary organizational skills. Susan Barry at McGraw-Hill must be thanked for her relentless editorial direction, as well as Howard Cohl at Affinity Communications Corp., who brought everyone together, and, last but not least, Nick DeLuca and Steve Bucher for their superior writing diligence.

Special thanks go to Judy Lugo, my administrative assistant, who took the scribble and made it legible.

Finally, while this book is a tribute to our collective corporate strength, it is in fact a fun way to explain the business casual phenomenon and guide businessmen through the process of dressing casually for success.

"Competition in the boardroom does not disappear with the removal of the jacket and tie."

Vice Chairmen
Phillips-Van Heusen

THE NEW RULES OF MEN'S FASHION

Fashion is a form of ugliness so intolerable that
we have to alter it every six months.

OSCAR WILDE

If you look good and dress well, you don't
need a purpose in life.

FASHION CONSULTANT ROBERT PANTE

There is no substitute for good taste.

MARK WEBER

How often do men shop for apparel?

Once a week (3%)
One to three times a month. (36%)
Once every 2-3 months (37%)
Twice a year (17%)
Once a year (7%)

(*Daily News Record* survey, Fairchild Publications)

As a society we are becoming more casual. Technology has allowed some of us to work out of our homes and to telecommute. The formal barriers between regions and countries have become smaller and smaller. The workplace is a much different place than it was 20 or even 10 years ago.

The good news about today's workplace is that men have a world of choices about what to wear to work. That's the bad news too—that men now have a world of choices about what to wear to work.

At one time, the man in the gray flannel suit, along with the man in the blue suit, the pinstriped suit, or even the Armani suit, ruled the business fashion world. Now he has been

The blue suit is no longer the norm.

joined by the man without a suit. Casual dressing has moved from the weekend into the work week. Pat Riley, coach of the NBA's Miami Heat, may still wear a suit courtside, but Larry Ellison, Oracle's CEO, appears in a turtleneck on bus stop ads. San Francisco's fashionable mayor, Willie Brown, may vow to send home anyone dressed casually on his staff, but one of the most important figures on the business scene today, Bill Gates, is rarely seen in a tie. And even IBM, which was the embodiment of the starched white shirt and tie, has allowed its workers to go casual.

All of this means that, while getting dressed for work was once as simple as opening the closet door, today there are decisions, decisions, decisions. There is the decision to dress formally or informally. If the choice is informal, there are decisions about what *sort* of casual look to wear: decisions on suit versus jacket, jacket versus sweater, tie versus collar or collarless shirt; decisions on slacks or twills or even jeans, sweaters or sweatshirts, socks or no socks.

What best suits a man at work often isn't a suit anymore, and the choice in the morning is now a lot more complicated than whether to wear a single- or double-breasted suit.

That's the bad news...

The good news is that, while getting dressed may have gotten harder, being dressed for work can now be a lot more fun, not to mention more comfortable, more productive, and even less expensive. Having choices that go beyond suit, shirt, and tie, that go beyond gray, navy, and white, that go beyond pinstripes and glen plaid—these all open up a world of possibilities for men in the workplace.

Casual dressing offers the chance (at least on certain days) to wear something comfortable in the place where you spend most of your waking hours, five days a week (or more). Casual dressing means that you can wear clothing that reflects more of the real world, not just the formal business world. Instead of packing you into a suit on the hottest day of the year, or buttoning up to the neck when you're trying to connect with a group of assembly line workers, you can allow what you wear to complement what you do. Casual dressing gives men the chance to be a little more of themselves on the job, to bring their own sense of style to

what they do as well as how they look—within limits, of course. And there's even evidence to show that dressing casually can help you get more work done and make you feel better while you do.

Of course, there are degrees of casual dressing styles. There is casual traditional (a polo shirt and khakis), dress (formal) casual traditional (an oxford shirt and khakis), casual (informal) contemporary (jeans and shirt), and dress casual contemporary (black slacks and black shirt), just to name a few.

But before going further into this brave new world of casual dressing, let's take a moment to look at what happened to the gray flannel suit.

The Passing of the Gray Flannel Suit

If you're old enough, you probably remember your father going off to work each day wearing much the same clothes every day. If he was an office worker, his uniform was a white shirt, tie, and suit. (Of course, there were quite a few *types* of suits, but, at the end of the day, a suit is a suit is a suit.) If he worked with his hands, his uniform might actually have been a uniform. Either way, back then you made a choice of work wear only once—when you chose a job.

If you're a little younger, you might remember a different sort of dad, whose uniform was a tie-dyed T-shirt, a pair of sandals, and jeans with patches sewn onto patches. The decision about what to wear to work still wasn't much of a decision, although in this case the reason might have been because your father's choice about work was not to.

And at some point in your career, one of these descriptions might have fit you as well as your father. Until recently, even if you decided to buck the trend, you'd be out of luck. There simply weren't many places to shop for business casual clothing other than the men's section on the fourth floor of a department store: "the suit department." The casual clothing you might have worn to play golf, to bowl, or to play some other sport was too far afield from acceptable wear in the office. It probably even seemed as if certain types of casual clothing, like jeans, weren't made for a man's body once he passed through his twenties. (Actually, the opposite is true.) Back then you had only a drawerful of old, battered jeans and T-shirts. You couldn't find the range of sweaters and blazers, shirts and shoes, vests and belts that today make it possible to put together a casual wardrobe. Stores like The Gap, clothing lines like Gant, and shoes like Bass Weejun "penny loafers" were at the beginning of that change, which has now remade the look of men's fashion in and out of the office.

The New Look of Business Casual Dress

There isn't just one "uniform" in the morning anymore

Whatever your age, if you're going off to work today, you know that the look at work has changed again. "What should I wear to work?" is now *really* a question. Unless you're throwing baserunners out from center field or fighting crime, you cannot put on just one uniform without question each morning.

And this new change is relatively recent. Just open the pages of John Malloy's *New Dress for Success,* which came out in 1988. Early in the book, you'll find this line: "The suit is the single most important garment worn by men ... it is the garment on which most people judge the wearer's status, character and abilities." But if you used that book today as

your guide, you'd find yourself clueless in ranking who's who at work, since in many offices, you won't find a suit anywhere from the front desk to the corner office.

The suit hasn't vanished, of course, but its role in the offices of many companies has certainly become less important (and more and more companies are going in this direction). On some days, the suit is nonexistent, depending on the industry, company, and locale. To track the changes, you should start with the baby boomers. In the 1980s, when members of that demographic juggernaut moved into middle age and middle management, they brought a different sensibility into the workplace. Suddenly a generation of employees, managers, and even owners didn't automatically trade in the clothes and habits of their youth when they passed the age of consent and picked up a college diploma. To be a "suit" was to be everything that the generation had rejected in its youth. With its newfound power, the boomers could choose to move into the work world without simply becoming a set of "suits," as so many of their fathers had done.

Maybe it was a prolonged attachment to the ways of their youth. Maybe it was that an increasing number of men were either unmarried or married to someone who also worked. (Incidentally, the appearance of more and more women in the office was another nudge away from the suit.) Or maybe it was just due to more and more time being spent commuting as well as working.

The result was a blurring of the separation between work and play, or between work and anything else. Men were less likely to go home first after work and change for a fancy evening out. Rather, they were more likely to go from work directly to some other activity. Thus, interest in clothing that would fit in more than one setting, or in clothing that would fit various lifestyles rose dramatically!

Today, many prominent businessmen are examples of this new suitless style. It's no accident that the likes of David Geffen and Bill Gates are leaders of companies at the forefront of today's corporate world.

Casual Dress and Corporate Success

The economy we know has a very different face from the economy our fathers knew. Products then were things you could hold in your hand or at least touch with your hand—products you could stamp out on an assembly line, as if the production process were run by a giant cookie cutter, rising and falling. Products now are often intangibles like information, and often producing those transparent products is itself an intangible process—the art of sitting in front of a computer and giving form to thought.

Just as a company of people who all think alike, work alike, and dress alike is unlikely to be a company headed for success in that new marketplace, a company whose people thrive under conditions of just-in-time production and meetings on-line is not likely to be a company of people who all find themselves fitting comfortably into pinstripes and gray flannel.

Many innovative companies (such as many of the high-tech firms) are leading the way in today's economy, putting more of a premium on what you produce, less on how you produce it. You don't get points anymore for just warming a chair eight hours a day (in fact, these days, you may not be going to the office to sit in a chair–period). And along with that shift in focus is a shift in what we wear at work. In fact, from a management point of view, the move to casual dressing says as well as anything else that results count.

It's a tough and competitive world. There is no longer time or room for nonsense and bureaucratic thinking. In a downsized world, the best minds need to be encouraged to excel and overachieve. Companies, shifting away from old norms, are finally focusing on value-added thinking. They realize that the failure to do so will only lead to their demise.

No matter how you analyze the benefits of casual dress, it's clear that the casual look has taken the corporate world

by storm, and it seems to be here to stay for a while. (Of course, there's no telling what fashion the next generation of executives will prefer.) Right now, nine out of ten companies have some form of casual dressing, from one day a week explicitly set aside for dressing down to five days a week, 52 weeks a year. The list of such companies is growing and includes IBM, Dun and Bradstreet, Burger King, Ford Motor Company, General Motors, and even Phillips-Van Heusen.

Also clear is that, whatever other ends casual dressing may serve, people just like it. Surveys conducted by the Daily News Record (DNR), one of the leading fashion trade publications, indicate that, given the chance, almost everyone takes advantage of a casual dress policy. Most employees think it's good for morale, and many of them think it's good for productivity. In the same survey, almost half said that, other things being equal, they'd choose a job with a company that had a casual dress policy over an offer from a suit-and-tie outfit.

In this book we'll look at the modern workplace and how business casual wear can fit into it appropriately. To some older readers, it may seem inconceivable that khakis could be worn to work. If you're younger, khakis might be acceptable, but you might not realize all your options in creating a casual wardrobe. Members of any generation will benefit from the tips in this book on how to take care of your clothes. At the end of this book, you'll find suggestions on how to create a casual dress code for your office.

As the DNR points out:

> *Despite the fact that three-quarters of the men [we] interviewed acknowledge they have a strong sense of personal style and can judge quality clothing, the study reveals that the male shopper needs help and knows it.*

So put on something comfortable, and let's enter the world of business casual wear.

1

CLOTHES 101

But he hasn't got anything on, a
little child said.

HANS CHRISTIAN ANDERSEN,
"The Emperor's New Cloths"

Nothing wears clothes, but Man.

GEORGE HERBERT

What men really think

The quality of high-priced clothing is superior to mid- or lower-priced apparel (49%).

Name brand clothing is assurance of quality and fashion. (62%).

(Responses are percentages of those surveyed.)

You should be aware of some clothing terminology. Here is a brief primer that has been divided into five categories:

✔ Fabrics

✔ Fibers

✔ Jackets

✔ Shirts

✔ Pants

If a term is used in the book that you don't understand, check back here. This list is by no means complete, but it should help you feel more at home when reading the rest of the book.

Fabrics

Chambray

A smooth, cotton fabric weaving white and color threads. It is shirt-weight denim, also called "denim-friendly" by some. It's longlasting and easy to care for. It usually comes prewashed. This is a versatile shirt fabric used for western shirts as easily as sport or dress shirts.

A collection of fabrics

Oxford

Oxford is a cotton fabric with a basketlike weave. It's heavier than most cotton blends. Oxford breathes well. It can be handwashed, although it's better to machine wash and line dry it. It is ideal for classic dress shirts and great for rough sport shirts. When ironing clothes made from it, turn them inside out.

Gingham

A cotton cloth, usually found in shirting stripes, checks, or plaids.

Herringbone

A type of weave found in men's jackets. The zig-zag pattern is supposed to resemble the skeleton of a herring. This pattern has gone in and out of style, although it's considered to be a classic weave. Herringbone was very popular in the 1940s.

Houndstooth

In this pattern, four light and four dark threads intertwine to create a checkered pattern. Traditionally it uses black and white threads. Usually the checkered pattern is smaller for men's clothes, larger for women's.

Tweed

Tweed is a coarse and checkered pattern. We get the term from the Scottish word *tweel,* which means "to cross." Tweed is used commonly in sports jackets, but it's not considered by many to be a dressy fabric.

Fiber

Cotton

Of all textiles sold, 47% of them are cotton. Moreover, its origins date back to 3000 B.C. Why? It's durable and it's the only fabric that gets stronger when it's wet, yet it can be waterproofed. However, it's not elastic or thermal. It's very versatile and can be worn in all seasons. Cotton stains very easily, though; so you need to remove any spots immediately. Cotton, because of its comfort, should be the foundation for a business casual wardrobe.

Wool

Wool is a soft, natural fiber. It is the most versatile fiber and its products can be used in extreme heat and cold, from the desert to the Arctic. It's fire resistant and absorbs water well. Wool will shrink, though, if washed incorrectly, as many first-time sweater owners will tell you. Therefore you should usually hand wash it. There are many varieties of

wool, including shetland, mohair, and angora. They really do get it from sheep (and some other animals, too).

Worsted Wool

A smooth but hard-twisted yarn-type material. It is made from combed wool.

Linen

This light and soft material is thought to be the oldest known fiber (older than cotton), and you'll find references to it in the Bible. Linen is a vegetable fiber from the flax plant. It wrinkles very easily; so iron it while it's damp. Try to avoid prolonged exposure to the sun since it's prone to fade. It's very strong and can withstand machine washing, but dry cleaning is recommended. Follow the old adage that says, "No linen before Memorial Day or after Labor Day." The adage, though, doesn't consider those who live in warmer climates; so feel free to wear it whenever you wish.

Silk

Silk is an elegant, dress-up fiber made from thin, shiny filaments from the silk worm. The Chinese have a saying: "Silk is the fabric you have to wear if you want to reach God." It is a good insulator; many clothes for camping and skiing are made with silk. It's a good idea to avoid prolonged exposure to sunlight. Silk is very susceptible to sweat and deodorant stains.

Polyester

A synthetic fiber, it is very strong and lasts a long time. Polyester can resist sunlight well and is easy to care for. In the past it hasn't been known to be very comfortable. This fiber got a bad rap in the 1970s as the uniform of disco, but because of recent innovations and microfiber high-twist variations, its use in performance sportswear and high fashion microfiber (expensive!) sportswear is experiencing a rebirth.

Jackets

Blazer

The blazer is the cornerstone jacket of business casual wear. Blazers can make jeans look respectable and flannel pants look less formal. Blazers are the traditional two-button jackets. While they can be double-breasted, brightly colored, or even emblazoned with a crest, the most common is navy blue single-breasted. A blazer and trousers should always contrast (not match).

The blazer is the cornerstone jacket

Lapels

In jackets, the lapels are usually about three to three and a half inches wide. Anything much more or less is entering a world of temporary relevance, and will not last the test of time.

Single-breasted

These jackets have two or three buttons and can be worn buttoned or unbuttoned.

Single-breasted jacket

Double-breasted

This type of jacket is usually worn (or should be worn) by men who are tall and thin because it adds about seven layers of fabric to their front. Double-breasted jackets should always be buttoned. They are much more formal and elegant than single-breasted jackets.

Shirts

Point Collar

Also known as the straight collar, the long, pointed collar is the most common type, and also has the most variations in length.

Button-down Collar

The two collar points button to the shirt. These relatively casual collars are much softer than other types. Button-down collars should play a large part in your business casual wardrobe.

*Top left: Banded collar. Top right: Button-down collar.
Bottom left: Point collar. Bottom right: Spread collar.*

Spread Collar

These shirts have a wider gap between the collar points than other shirts, and the collars are very rigid. They are used in European suits. Spread collars are meant to be worn with a tie.

Banded Collar

The collar band without the collar. Until this century, all men's shirts had banded collars and would come with detachable collars. Recently, some of the sartorially bold have been wearing banded collar shirts with tuxedos. Banded collars were very popular on Nehru jackets, for those of you old enough to remember Nehru jackets.

Crew Neck

A roundish, tight fitting neckline. This is the more commonly seen collar on sweaters and T-shirts.

Polo

Not just a game, but a pullover sport shirt, usually knitted. This is the classic short-sleeved casual shirt, such as the Izod classic knit shirt. It allows you a lot of shoulder and back movement. Hence its popularity on the golf course.

Turtleneck

While this is normally thought of as a very high-necked sweater (which it is) there are also turtleneck cotton shirts. Its name is rather obvious to anyone who's tried one on.

A note on cuffs: Cuffs are fairly stable, although they vary widely for knits—either open sleeve or ribbed knit. However, for dress shirts, there is a very formal style found in the "French cuff." French cuffs are shirt cuffs that fold over. They have four button holes but no buttons. Cufflinks are needed when you wear French cuffs.

Pants

Khakis

These pants are made from khaki cloth (twills). They're usually found in beige or tan, and they are similar to chinos. This is a main staple in the business casual wardrobe. Khakis were developed from military uniforms; British army officers would often wear khakis when off duty (hence the term "khaki officer").

Chino

A cotton fabric in a firm weave. Basically, chinos are very similar to khakis, but are woven tighter and are often lighter in weight. They're usually found in beige or tan. Chinos can have plain fronts or be pleated.

Denim

This is the material blue jeans are made from. The fabric is made from cotton and is very resilient. The word *jeans* comes from Genoese sailors who wore pants made of denim. (It's not known if they also wore denim jackets.)

Twill

Twill is a type of fabric made from combed yarn. It's not elastic and gets shiny after repeated wearing (depending on the tightness of the weave). Twill hides dirt well; so you don't have to clean it as often. When you do, you should dry clean it. It breathes well. 100 % cotton twills are the foundation of a corporate casual wardrobe.

Appropriate pants

Flannel

Flannel, made from a soft, loosely woven wool cloth, provides wonderful ventilation and avoids creasing well. It can be made in different weights for different seasons. You should only dry clean flannel. When ironing it, turn the pant leg inside out. Casual dressers usually feel very comfortable in a gray flannel slacks.

Corduroy

Corduroy, taken from a French word meaning "court of the king," was once known as the velvet of the poor. It is made from cotton. Its ridges are a cushion of air, making it the warmest of the cotton materials. So it's usually a winter fabric.

Worsted Wool Gabardine

A high twist, wool fabric, light in weight, yet correct all year round. It's usually a formal fabric and pant, yet it is great for formal casual!

Pant Detailing

Pleats

These are the folds in the front of pants, usually two or three on each side of the zipper. Pleats make the fabric hang much better on you, although it's up to your individual

taste. Pleats provide extra fabric for you which is required when you move or sit. Most wool and linen pants come with pleats. Comfort, again, is the key, with an added by-product being good looks. Pleats, by the way, can also be found in some shirts to provide extra room for moving and stretching.

Cuffs

Pant cuffs are usually about one and a half inches wide. They were supposedly invented by Edward VIII, who rolled up his pants so that they wouldn't get muddy. In Europe, the standard cuff falls to just below the top of the shoe. Americans tend to wear them a bit higher. (We love cuffs.)

Now that you are familiar with the terms used in the clothing industry, let's see how some of them can make their way into a business casual wardrobe.

2

IMAGE IS EVERYTHING

If I am what I wear, then what should I wear?
ANONYMOUS

Anything you can wear, I can wear better.
IRVING BERLIN, "Annie Get Your Gun"

Well done is better than well said.
BENJAMIN FRANKLIN

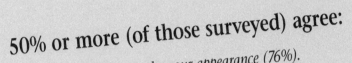

50% or more (of those surveyed) agree:

People judge you by your appearance (76%).

Clothing reflects my status in life (59%).

Call it the new PC—professional correctness. Casual dressing doesn't mean anything goes. In fact, it's harder than ever before for men to know what is appropriate to wear in the workplace and what's not. No more going to the best store you can afford and bringing home a stack of white shirts, a pile of muted ties, a dark suit, and black shoes (not to mention a whopping credit card bill). You do have choices, lots of choices, but not limitless ones. Just remember that the rules for conducting yourself sartorially at work are different now, but never make the mistake of assuming that there are no rules.

In some companies today—maybe a handful—what you wear doesn't matter a bit. The odds are, though, that you work in a place where what you wear is noticed and what you wear counts. And unless you're the office Einstein, wearing mismatched socks is unlikely to be your ticket up through the ranks.

In the old days, you made your statement through clothing by not making a statement. Like a chameleon's skin, the purpose of a suit and tie was to allow you to blend in, to be one of the guys. It was *not* to make you noticed. The suit and tie were a standard issue for every male worker; you donned them when you enlisted.

It's often said that the business world can be like war, and the suit and tie constituted the battle uniform that every good soldier wore. This went for everyone from the privates at their desks to the generals in the boardroom. If your uniform didn't look like everyone else's, you weren't a team player.

Today, that's only half true. The function of what you wear to work is still to fit in, but there is a wider range of possibilities for fitting in. Yes, you have an opportunity for self-expression now. Yes, you have an opportunity to be more comfortable on the job. And yes, your casual clothes at work still have to fit your company's image. So your job is not to define casual dressing in your workplace; rather it is to find a way of expressing your company's definition of casual dressing.

The WYSIWYG Approach

Casual dressing has more than one definition. It means different things to different companies. Casual dressing at IBM is unlikely to be the same as casual dressing at *Wired* magazine. The best criteria for determining what fits your company's definition and what doesn't is WYSIWYG (which, if you're not up on your computer terminology, is a mnemonic for "what you see is what you get" and is pronounced "whiz-e-wig"). Look around the office and see what other people are wearing. If you don't see any high-tops, the odds are that Nike is not the brand of footwear you should be shopping for before you start that new job. If you see turtlenecks but no T-shirts, plan on keeping that "number 23" basketball jersey in the dresser drawer until Saturday. Even if you work in the mailroom, your first assignment as a new employee is not likely to be pushing the fashion envelope.

Pay attention. In the workplace there's no need to be a fashion pioneer. You're unlikely to find your way to the top hastened by the fact that you were the first person in the office to wear an electric blue body hugging T-shirt. It's just fine to introduce that new look gradually. Especially cautious individuals can always resort to the traditional guide to corporate behavior: Follow the boss. (Of course, if your boss is a woman, you'll have to look at where her wardrobe falls

in the range of women's fashion, and then translate it to men's dress. But you'll still find plenty of clues in color choices, fabric types, and the like.)

Your Peers

Another way to gauge what is acceptable is to look at how your peer group dresses. Usually, those who occupy positions of equal stature tend to dress alike. This is a phenomenon we at Van-Heusen have noticed over the years (although with the growing acceptance of corporate casual wear, this is becoming even more difficult). If you were to take a random group of people from a street in Manhattan at lunchtime and put them in one room, you'd probably be able to tell what occupation or level of seniority most of them had by how they were dressed. Midlevel managers have a certain look, entry-level workers have another, lawyers yet another. This is, of course, partly due to the fact that every group has its own income level, which has a lot to do with what types of clothes they can afford. Of course, there are exceptions.

But it also is a reflection of the corporate culture that has been established over the years at a given company. (One company president told us that, at one time upon elevation to senior manager level, men were rewarded with a pair of suspenders to signify their ascent. This is an extreme example, but it illustrates the importance of clothing in corporate culture.)

Using Common Sense

Remember that in the postsuit era, no single look is appropriate. In every workplace, a range of casual dress works. If you feel unsure of yourself, generally speaking you can't do any harm by sticking to the more conservative end of the range. But it's actually not that hard to identify the basic do's and don'ts of casual dressing at work. You'll find that, for the most part, the guidelines are simply common sense.

One guideline that screams of common sense is that whatever you wear should be clean and neat. This might seem obvious, but remember that, when choosing a business casual look, you're wearing clothes to work that you may be accustomed to wearing in very different settings. It's unlikely you'd find yourself buttoning up a white shirt with a huge ketchup stain over the pocket or pulling on a pair of cotton sweatpants worn through at the knee while dressing for work. However, you might well be used to wearing a T-shirt with a blotch of motor oil on it or a pair of jeans torn in the rear while at home. Different places, different rules. Neatness does count, even in business casual wear.

There are also styles of casual clothing—sleeveless T-shirts or biking shorts—that almost never work at work.

Form follows function. Think about what you do at work and what you have to do on a given day. The same jeans and (nice) T-shirt that might work just fine for a day spent

doing layout on your computer would probably be a bad idea for a meeting with the clients for whom you're doing the work. If you spend your day near the front desk and are visible to all who visit the company, you are part of their first impression of the entire company. It's unlikely that a baseball cap and work boots create the image most businesses want to project, though it might be just fine in the graphics department. A crisply pressed shirt, light khakis, and loafers would probably do the trick instead.

Your own image may need to change from day to day, or even in the course of the day. If Friday includes lunch with prospective business partners, your wardrobe for the day may include a jacket and/or tie. If Thursday takes you to the bank, you might choose a suit for that more traditional setting. You may even have to keep a second jacket in the office just in case your role changes during the day. On the other hand, you might work for a company that deliberately cultivates a hip, even in-your-face style, in which case the only jacket you might hang on your door would be leather. Today, businessmen often have to play more than one role and fit into more than one image.

But these images are only part of the overall picture. The most important thing to remember about dressing casually at work is that the company's image comes before your image. Whether you're applying for a job or you already have one, you want to be part of your work team. That means

what you wear, no less than how you act, should work for the greater good, not against it. Your wardrobe at work isn't intended to show that you're on the cutting edge at the expense of the job to be done.

But that doesn't mean the old dress code has simply given way to a new, equally rigid set of rules. On most jobs, the appropriate wardrobe is a range of styles, and styles may overlap between jobs. A designer and an account executive may both wear the same blazer, but the designer would add a dash of panache by wearing that jacket over a cotton T-shirt, while the account executive would toe the line a little more by wearing a banded-collar woven shirt instead.

How Far Is Far Enough?

In general, a quick check in the mirror each morning should be enough to tell you if you're on the right track. If you look like you're dressed to go somewhere other than work, you probably aren't dressed for work. A sleeveless T-shirt with a pair of cutoffs and sandals belong in the park or at the beach, not at the office. The clothes you wear to garden or to paint on the weekend should stay home Monday morning when you head off to work.

This may seem like common sense, but too many times we've seen employees take the notion of a "casual day" a bit too far. One employee we know equated the casual look with

the "unshaven, rolled-out-of-bed look." While most dress-down days are in place to boost morale, in the end, business is still business. Something that's inappropriate outside the workplace is even less appropriate in the office.

The Cost of the Casual Look

If you think about it, though, humorous T-shirts and sweatpants aren't the only types of casual clothes you already have at home. One of the pleasant discoveries about casual dress is that you probably already have some of what you'll need in your closet, even if you've never gone shopping for casual work clothes. Jackets, blazers, and shirts that have been in your closet for years may work together, even though you didn't realize that when you purchased them.

There are other perks to the trend. A casual wardrobe for work is usually less expensive than the old suit and tie, which is another nice boost for morale—except when you first realize that your "traditional" wardrobe is dated and you need to invest more in your look. And, as you probably know, you get what you pay for. You can buy well made casual clothing at a variety of prices and it's probably money well spent. Even in a casual look, you can notice the difference between quality and "bargains."

Still, compared to a formal wardrobe, you'll be saving money from the basic price of purchasing the clothes to ex-

penses like dry cleaning. If you're just starting out or you're working your way up the corporate hierarchy, you'll find that filling the closet with a casual business wardrobe is less expensive than buying more formal clothes.

However, consider one more extremely important factor when deciding to "upgrade" your wardrobe to a casual style: Women purchase 70% of all men's clothes! So be sure that your new sense of what is casually correct to you is properly conveyed to the woman in your life. You can do this by window shopping together, commenting on newspaper and magazine ads, and even discussing fashion while watching the latest programs on television (although actually only a small percentage of men actually watch TV or view movies to see what latest fashions are in).

The Many Casual—
Not So Casual—Images

The most important question to ask yourself before you invest in a business casual wardrobe is whether you're the type who *wants* to dress casually at work. You may be of the old school and think that it's inappropriate to wear anything other than a suit when doing business. Your personality may be such that you like how a suit makes you feel. You may not even be the type who *should* dress casually.

That's fine. In fact, if you don't feel comfortable wearing a certain type of jacket to the office, then by all means don't. There's nothing worse than trying to be someone you're not. Most people in business can see right through you when you put up a facade.

So you need to be honest with yourself about the image you want to project through your clothing. And there are just as many clothing personality types as there are types of clothing. Here are a few we've noticed over the years, the names of which we've made up for convenience. (If you happen to fall into one of them, that's okay, but don't feel that you have to be this way forever. While it's necessary to be yourself you also have to stretch once in a while.)

The Old School

If you're a member of The Old School, then this book may not be for you. This is the kind of man who may just sleep in a suit; he feels naked in the business world without one. He loves to accessorize: He'll wear cufflinks, tie pins, and a color-coordinated handkerchief poking neatly out of his jacket's breast pocket. The Old School dresser doesn't have to have an expensive wardrobe. He feels just that his clothes should reflect his duties: formal and efficient. And just because he's called the Old School, don't assume that he's old. He can very easily be a 25-year-old with an MBA.

Status Quo

The Status Quo type is the picture of consistency. He might seem to wear the same thing every day. He's neither natty nor a poor dresser. His suit is neatly pressed, and his shirt is noticeably starched. Change is not his friend. He sees no reason to change since he's comfortable in what he's wearing. And while the Old School likes to add frills to complement his style, the Status Quo will have none of that. He believes in the effectiveness of wardrobe austerity. In truth, he doesn't really want to put a lot of thought or effort into what he wears. On occasion, the Status Quo dresses casually, usually on a holiday when his presence in the office beckons.

The Fashion Victim

The Fashion Victim knows what's being worn in Paris, New York, and Milan. If there's a trend out there, he'll find it. Usually the Fashion Victim makes his living in an industry that encourages such—well—hipness, such as entertainment, advertising, etc. Being the Fashion Victim doesn't always make you laughable, however. In fact, the Fashion Victim puts a lot of thought into what he wears and it usually pays off. It gets exhausting, though, keeping up with the ever-changing styles.

The Chameleon

The Chameleon is adept at changing his style to match whatever he's going to be doing that day. He is equally comfortable dressing in a three-piece suit for a presentation one day and then rolling up the sleeves of his denim jacket the next to inspect an on-site project. He doesn't like to stay with one style for too long; otherwise he starts to feel fenced in.

Mr. Casual

Mr. Casual is a very easygoing person, not given to fits of anger or stress, and his personality is reflected in his clothes and in how he wears them. He'll show up to work sometimes with his tie already loosened at the neck. Most of his clothes are loose fitting. If his tie is a bit long or if his shoes are a bit scuffed, he won't throw a tantrum. Mr. Casual could be seen as sloppy by some, simply unpretentious by others. He is, perhaps, a bit *too* casual.

The New Guard

In contrast to the Old School, who feels right at home in his precise pinstripes and polished shoes, the New Guard is similar in that he's comfortable with his look. He's also similar to Mr. Casual, but the New Guard wouldn't tolerate his khakis being wrinkled or his tie having an espresso stain. He believes that his clothes should reflect his professionalism, but he also wants to be comfortable.

As you might have concluded by now, dressing casually can work at the office if it's done professionally and confidently. You may or may not fit any of these personality types, or you may be a combination of several, but one of the goals of this book is to bring out at least a little of the New Guard in you. The hope is that you'll start to be aware of your own clothing personality and the effect it can have on those around you. One way to see this is by trying to recognize the image that is projected by your clothes. Remember, there is no substitute for good taste.

3

YOUR IMAGE

Image is everything.
ANDRE AGASSI, Canon advertisements

Clothes make the man. Naked people have
little or no influence on society.
MARK TWAIN

50% or more (of those surveyed) agree:

I like to have someone with me when I shop (46%).

No matter how much I like an item, I wait until it's on sale (30%).

I have a strong sense of personal style (75%).

Designers in the clothing business years ago had it easy. To think up designs for working men, all they had to do was to picture a certain type of worker. If they thought of a banker, they knew that bankers had a specific look. If they thought of a salesman, they could design a look that they knew would suit most salesmen. There was an abundance of fashion clichés and stereotypes. They probably could tell a person's occupation by seeing what they wore on the bus, train, or subway.

Today, though, as business casual spreads, it's much more difficult to know what people do for a living based solely on their clothes. The influence of business casual wear can be seen across the board. Almost any business today allows its employees to wear more casual clothes to some extent, thus blurring the stereotypical sartorial lines we have come to know.

If you don't believe us, take the following Image Ink Blot test. Here are ten different looks. These are real looks from real people that we've put together based on interviews and magazines, including such business publications as *Fortune.* As you go through this list, think about what type of professional might wear the clothes described. You might also picture someone wearing these combinations where you work or imagine yourself in these clothes. The chances are that you'll match some looks immediately to some of the choices, but others won't be so simple.

Here's how it works. First we'll give you a list of nine looks. You'll then be given a list of nine occupations. Your job is to match the look to the occupation.

THE LOOKS   OCCUPATION

1. Black jeans, black silk shirt, black belt _____

2. T-shirt, faded jeans, brown belt, earring _____

3. Sport shirt, shorts, and sandals _____

4. Suit jacket, white shirt, maroon tie, and
   a pair of army fatigue pants _____

5. Navy Izod shirt, gray worsted wool slacks _____

6. Pressed Gant oxford shirt, jeans, and
   penny loafers (no socks) _____

7. Custom-fit suit, tie _____

8. Sport jacket, white buttoned-down shirt,
   striped tie _____

9. Khaki pants, buttoned-down beige shirt in a
   patterned weave, beige T-shirt underneath _____

10. Knit collar shirt with crested logo, color-
    coordinated slacks, matching sweater vest
    with similar logo _____

Now look at the list of occupations and try to match up the people with the previous looks.

THE OCCUPATIONS

A. President, snow-boarding company
B. Security officer
C. CEO, computer company
D. VP, major auto maker
E. Conservative political activist
F. Corporate marketing manager, clothing company
G. Chairman, major film company
H. Wall Street financier
I. Software guru, silicon valley
J. Professional golfer

Let's see how you did.

✔ *Number 1* was black on black on black. That is occupation G, the Hollywood look. An easy one to start with.

✔ *Number 2* is A, the thirty-something president of the snow boarding company.

✔ *Number 3*—How did you do with this one? It's not so obvious. The answer is I, a cybernaut from silicon valley.

✔ *Number 4* is a bit of a trick question. The answer is E, and the explanation is that he was dressing for television from the waist up and for comfort (David Letterman pre-CBS) (or maybe political warfare) from the waist down.

✔ *Number 5* is D, at least some of the time. When that VP heads off to the shop floor, he leaves the jacket and tie at home.

✔ *Number 6* is C, but don't jump to conclusions. This company happens to be one of the country's big names in PCs, not a little multimedia start-up in somebody's basement. (It also happens to be in Texas, where it's hot.)

✔ *Number 7*, the custom suit, you might have pegged as Wall Street. So if you said H, you were right.

✔ *Number 8*—what did you make of this one? It is B, because the security officer was dressing against the image of the job. Looking like a cop was the last thing he wanted.

✔ *Number 9,* that classic business casual outfit, was, in fact, someone who worked for a company that makes casual business clothing: answer F.

✔ *Number 10,* what else but the pro golfer? The answer is J.

Some of the answers were pretty obvious, but even the matches that might seem unpredictable at first glance often make sense when you fit them into context. They may not fit your abstract image of a profession, but they make sense when you think about the requirements of the profession (and, in particular, of the person). If you work, for example, at a law firm in Hawaii, wearing a tie might make you look good, but it certainly won't make you feel good. (Actually, a Hawaiian lawyer often wears a flowered shirt, except when he's in court.) That is what business casual wear is all about.

If you're in senior management with an industrial company and you've got to sit down and talk with unionized production workers, the traditional gray flannel suit is like a suit of armor. This prevents contact between employer and employees, which is the last thing you want in that situation. And a security officer who wants to accomplish his job through respect rather than force doesn't always want to look like he just jumped out of a SWAT team helicopter. What you wear and how you wear it sends signals. So you want to be sure you know what your clothes are saying, and you want to be sure that's what you mean to say.

Clothing as a Message

Business casual wear can be functional if it sends the right message. Once upon a time, a suit sent the only message a white collar worker needed, but times have changed. By putting on a polo shirt, the auto industry vice president can say he is not a stuffed shirt. He can bridge some of the distance between his office and the shop floor by what he wears.

When that same VP meets with his company's bankers, putting them at ease probably still calls for wearing a pin-striped suit, instead of gray flannel slacks. But just as a suit can be reassuring in one setting, in another your business casual wear might put a client or partner at ease. If somebody on the creative side at a hip local ad agency showed up for a meeting in a three-piece, pin-striped suit, would he be saying "current" and "creative" to you? No. That's because the three-piece suit is not intended to give that message, but almost exactly the opposite message. It says "tradition," it says "stability," it emphasizes your ties to the past, rather than to the future. If you're selling contemporary, you'd better look a little contemporary.

In short, when you dress to send a message, you're dressing for somebody else. If you look like a teenager, you're more likely to be treated like a teenager, and in a business meeting, that's unlikely to be a recipe for success. So think twice before you ask that kid on the skateboard where he got the Jams.

What's in It for Me?

It can't be emphasized enough that, when going casual, you have to keep in mind what message you want to send. This, however, is considering only half the people involved. In every message there are two parties: the receiver and the sender. So far we've seen the influence that business casual wear can have on receivers. It can make them more receptive to your message.

But what about the sender? What about you? What do *you* get out of business casual wear?

The most important benefit is that it's comfortable. It isn't just a matter of loosening a tie that cuts off the blood to your brain or taking off your jacket on a hot summer's day. Business casual wear is made differently. You'll find softer fabrics, more natural shapes, and room to move. It's comfortable because it's designed to be that way. (In contrast, one executive at a company that makes dress shirts says, "There is nothing more barbaric than a dress shirt, nothing more professional.") Business casual strikes a middle ground between the hip-hugging jeans you wore in college and the boxy suits of the 1980s that swallowed up a man's body.

This allows you as the sender of business messages to be more effective. Being comfortable has a positive psychological effect on people's ability to communicate well. And since communication is vital to every job in the working world,

it's no wonder that more and more companies are allowing a casual dress code. They know that their employees perform better in most business scenarios when they are physically comfortable. In the final analysis it just makes more sense.

We'll look at a few of these scenarios in Chapter 4.

4

WHAT TO WEAR WHEN...

Beware of all enterprises requiring new clothes.
HENRY DAVID THOREAU

I don't know the key to success, but the key to
failure is trying to please everyone
ANONYMOUS

Where men look for information on men's apparel fashions

Window shopping (33%)   Newspaper ads (19%)
Circulars (14%)   Magazine ads (10%)
Catalogs (9%)   Friends (8%)
TV (7%)   Movies (1%)

Frequency of purchasing brand name apparel

Always (27%)   Sometimes (53%)
Seldom (17%)   Never (2%)

Before we continue, let's see how you do on a brief true or false quiz. Circle True or False, depending on what you think the correct answer must be.

True or False? 1. You should never consider who you'll be meeting with when planning how to dress for work.

True or False? 2. Where you conduct business should have no effect on how you dress.

True or False? 3. The time of day should have no bearing on what you wear.

True or False?   4. Businessmen in every country take the same approach to business casual wear.

True or False?   5. Your clothes probably do not affect the outcome of a job interview.

The answers are provided at the end of the chapter, but by that time you'll have answered them anyway.

This chapter covers some situations in which you might not be sure how to dress casually. Once we get outside the safe and familiar confines of the traditionally attired office, we have to play by different rules. There is a place for business casual wear out there in the real world. The trick is to know beforehand what to expect and how to prepare your wardrobe accordingly. Keep in mind the cardinal rule: Be honest with yourself, and dress in a way that makes you feel comfortable with who you are.

... You're Taking Care of Business, Outside the Office

In talking on the phone with a vice president of a major Midwestern brewing company, he laughed when we asked him what he was wearing that day. A suit and tie, he said, but what was funny was that he'd just returned from a business meeting where the people he was meeting with were all dressed casually (obviously he was expecting a more formally dressed greeting). However, it's also not unusual to find that people dress up to meet each other, even when both companies involved have casual dress policies. This is because people aren't sure what casual dress means outside their own companies.

In days gone by, when all white-collar workers wore jackets and ties, there was no such indecision. In days to come, if all white-collar workers opt for business casual wear, that won't happen either. But today, when we have one foot (or one dress shoe) in the old world and one foot (or one loafer) in the new, the question of what to wear for business meetings is not as simple to answer as it was in the past.

No book can give you a hard and fast answer for every situation that might come up. One approach is to ask yourself specific questions about the situation you're going into. As you might know, reporters always ask basic questions of any potential news story. By answering the five W's—who, what, when, where, and why—reporters know what information needs to be included in the story. The same is true when trying to decide which casual wear is appropriate in a given situation. So by answering the 5 W's, you have a good idea how to prepare your casual wardrobe for any situation.

Who is the meeting with? When is the meeting? Where is the meeting? What is the meeting about? Why are you have a meeting? Once you've answered these questions, you should be ready to step over to the closet and dress for the job.

Who?

Who will be at the meeting? Are you meeting with your boss? Your colleagues? Your subordinates? If the meeting is with people outside your company, are you meeting potential clients for the first time or checking in with long-time customers? Are you meeting with people in a line of work that's likely to have a significantly different corporate culture?

One of the most important skills in knowing what to wear is the same skill that is generally necessary in business: audience analysis. You have to know who you're dealing with, so that you'll know what to say, how to act, and what to wear. You have to know if your audience is going to be above or below you on the hierarchical ladder. You have to know if they're from your company or from a different company with different rules. How you answer these questions will factor in to what you will wear.

Once again, it's important to consider a company's corporate culture. The corporate culture is the personality of a company, which is made up of its traditions and values. Just like people, no two companies have the same personality. And since an individual's personality dictates what he will wear, so too will a corporate culture determine how the employees of a company will dress. This is usually found explicitly in a company's dress code (discussed in greater length at the end of this book), but sometimes a dress code is more suggested than formal. So knowing the corporate

culture of a company helps you with your audience analysis. To be forewarned when it comes to your attire is to be forearmed. And when your audience's culture clashes with yours, it's always best to defer to their style of dress.

When?

When is the meeting? Is it midday or after work? Are you having breakfast, lunch, or dinner together? The key to dressing for any meeting during business hours is knowing what's appropriate for the other person. For a conservative client or a first-time sales pitch, you would probably dress more conservatively, subject, of course, to your answers to the who and the why questions. Your answers to those questions may dictate that, because of the message you are trying to send, such conservative attire may be equally inappropriate. An ad agency executive seeking to convey a with-it message is an ideal example.

For a meeting with a long-time client, you would already know what to wear. (The when question in this case also applies to how many times you've met someone before.)

What about after-work meetings? In the old days, a meeting over dinner, or anywhere else after work, might have required a change of clothes. More than likely, your traditional business wear would have been either too dressy or not dressy enough, depending on whether the entertainment for a client was formal or just a dinner at a funky local restau-

rant. Dressed casually for the office, you might find a simple change will do just fine. You might, for example, take off your tie (for a more casual look) or throw on the jacket that you've kept hanging on the back of your office door all day. You might change from deck shoes to lace-ups, or vice-versa if your destination is a bit more dress-up. Or you might trade that buttoned-down shirt for a cotton T-shirt under your jacket, if the occasion is more contemporary casual.

Another "when" to consider is the season. Certainly during the winter, for example, there would be a lot more understanding if you showed up at a meeting wearing a sweater vest.

"When" might also apply to weather conditions, such as rain or snow. Not a lot of meetings take place in the park, but you'd be surprised how forgiving executives can be when people arrive at a conference or meeting having battled the elements.

Where?

Where is the meeting? Are you inviting someone to your office or meeting at someone else's? Is the meeting out in the field or "out in the field"? Are you meeting at a diner or an elegant restaurant? If the meeting is at a traditional restaurant, such as an old-fashioned steak house, you want to dress the part. It could mean something from the conservative business casual side of the closet, like a navy blazer, gray wool slacks, and tassel loafers. If the meeting is in the field,

take the conditions into account. You don't have to go like a construction worker, for example, to visit a construction site. But you might replace the loafers with a pair of work boots or rugged outdoor shoes and leave the fine wool jacket at home in favor of something a bit more rugged, like a washed cotton twill.

Generally, what to wear and where to go usually go hand in hand. If the client chooses the location, then dressing for the restaurant, for example, is the same as dressing for the client. But if *you* choose the location, you want a setting where you *and* your client will be comfortable. So, unless you and your Wall Street banker are also good buddies, you don't take him to your favorite fast food dive or to the newly opened Third Wave California cuisine stop where everyone in the room is under thirty.

Another "where" to consider is where in the world. Many businesses today have expanded globally due to favorable trade agreements, so you need to know about the foreign land you might be visiting, along with the fashion requirements to meet or mistakes to avoid. Keep an open mind. Ours is only one culture on this planet, and how we dress, casually or otherwise, is by no means the only way. What passes for casual wear here might be seen as something entirely different in other countries. (There are specific examples later in this chapter.) A red tie might signify power in this country, but may have a more amorous meaning overseas.

The goal is to avoid "sartorial ethnocentrism." That's a polysyllabic way of saying, "Respect how other cultures dress." A preparatory call ahead can go a long way.

What and Why?

What's the purpose of the meeting? *Why* is it being held? Are you trying to get someone's business, or are you being pursued? Do you need to set people at ease or impress them? Are you the buyer or the seller? Are you going over routine matters or into serious negotiations? Is the tenor of the meeting likely to be friendly or hostile? In an established relationship, you have no question about what to wear, and what you wear does not make as much of a difference. But keep in mind that casual dressing is fun. So, in addition to being conscious of the professionalism of your appearance, *have fun!* The golden rule of the five W's is to call ahead to either learn or coordinate policy between you and your client. With that in mind, let's look at a few scenarios where you might really need to dress a part.

Scenario 1

Suppose you're meeting with a prospective client who is interested in you because he or she wants a more contemporary look in the company's print advertising campaign. You don't want to lay it on too thick, but dressing on the stylish, casual side reinforces your message in an unspoken fashion: You are the person to hire for that late twentieth-century look.

What do you wear? You have a variety of options, many of which are appropriate:

✔ Casual traditional (e.g., Izod shirt and khakis)

✔ Dress casual traditional (e.g., Oxford shirt and khakis)

✔ Casual contemporary (e.g., jeans and a black shirt)

✔ Dress casual contemporary (e.g., black slacks and a black shirt).

Be careful and sensitive to cross-over dressing, which is mixing the traditional and contemporary, and the casual and the dress casual. (The difference between casual and dress casual is really a matter of degree.) Sometimes cross-over dressing works, but it really depends on how you answer the five W's. When cross-over dressing, you might choose a cotton T-shirt or a banded collar shirt and black slacks (the David Geffen look), but you'd be unlikely to choose a polo shirt or a traditional buttoned-down look with tie. You'd probably leave the tweed jacket and the navy blazer at home in favor of something with a more subtle texture—maybe a silk/wool blend or a linen, and maybe something with a bit of color in it. You might choose a pair of pants with a tight solid texture or something in the way of a dressy wool slack, rather than khakis.

Scenario 2

You're headed into a tough negotiating session. If you see yourself as the underdog or as the person who is asking for something, you might consider dressing in a more authoritative fashion: dark colors, a traditional look, with jacket and pants in complementary colors, something wool with a substantial feel to it (no denims or linens), a tie in a muted color or pattern, and a pair of loafers or lace-ups. On the other hand, if you come into a situation as the "heavy," you might want to dress against the type. As the boss, for example, you might want to wear something more informal, a tweed or herringbone jacket, a tie, a pair of khakis or a pair of dark cotton slacks. These are all examples of a disarming gesture.

Scenario 3

You're meeting with someone you don't know from another company. Call ahead. It's not unusual for suppliers to check with us before a visit to see if the people they will be visiting will be dressing casually or not. As long as there are different standards in different companies, you have no way of knowing what you're walking into. If you're concerned that what you walk in wearing might influence the outcome, call ahead.

... You're on the Road

Over the last twenty or thirty years, a lot of the regional differences within the United States have been swept away. You'll find McDonald's and Kinko's, Pepsi and Coke, IBM and

HP just about everywhere these days. Technology, especially, has made the United States one large region at times.

The same is true of fashion. Where once there might have been distinct regional styles, that's much less true today in the United States. Now you dress more for the occasion and less for the destination. What's more important about your meeting is whether it's with your ad agency or your bankers, not whether it's in Pittsburgh or Pensacola.

For business overseas, however, you should know a few things. Oddly enough, in both Europe and Asia the standards for business are both more formal and more relaxed than they are here.

Let's talk about formality first. In Europe, being formal is stylish. You'll find a contemporary look: suits that are styled, jackets and ties with bold patterns and colors and textures, shirts with color rather than plain white. In Asia, formal is traditional. There your suit should be serious, in dark and muted colors. You would even do just fine in a double-breasted suit.

At the same time, our counterparts overseas are more casual about their casual wear. In Italy, for example, you'll find your white-collar colleagues entirely at home in a silk T-shirt, jeans, and boots. On the continent (Western Europe), men have a more developed sense of style than you're probably accustomed to here. So keep your eyes open, and you'll learn a few things. In Asia, you'll find casual can be just plain casual—sometimes very sloppy (as you'll see if you get a chance to observe an overseas office when they're not dressing up for you), particularly in Hong Kong and Taiwan. Of course, the heat and the disparate stages of economic development are two important factors that account for this trend. Japan and Korea, on the other hand, are the bastions of formality. Navy or gray suits, no substitutes.

Wherever your business travels might take you, here's a tip. New fabrics—wools and blends that have been appearing on the market—are, if not wrinkle-free, at least pretty close. You can actually wear your suit on the plane and get off looking as though you just put it on. While the better ones are costly, if you travel a lot, you might find one of those suits worth the money. They are a sure way to be casually correct when you travel. (We'll get into more depth on travel later in the book.)

... You're Interviewing for a Job

Most of what you need to know about dressing to get a job is the same as dressing for a job you already have. It always helps to have a picture—literally—of your prospective employer's corporate culture. By poking your head in the office, looking through pictures in the annual report, asking the receptionist on the phone something about how people dress, you'll be able to dress appropriately. Just add what people wear to the list of topics you research about a prospective employer before you go for the interview.

If you want to stand out, it's generally better to err on the formal side. Almost always, it's better to be a little over-dressed than a little underdressed for an interview. As for colors, check the section of this book on color for specific tips.

Above all, don't think of the interview as a psychodrama in which your red tie compels the interviewer to hire you or your blue shirt sets her at ease. You can use color only to add a little edge to your personality or subtract a little from it. People generally see dark colors as projecting power and competency, and light colors as friendly. So you might consider tempering your personality a bit one way or the other. For example, if you tend to intimidate people, or come on a little strong, you might move out of the navy/black range and into something in the grays. The navy suit, white shirt, and classic tie always works for the formal approach. A navy blazer, white buttoned-down oxford shirt, khakis, and loafers always works for casual dress. For other approaches, keep reading.

You'd be surprised how often candidates for a job forget about the details of their appearance. A splendidly put-to-gether outfit can be undone in a moment by little things, like shoes that are unshined or are worn down at the heels. Perhaps, in the great scheme of things, it's not so important if your hair is all over the place or you haven't washed your hands. But in an interview—in that moment of making a first impression—it can be deadly. So take a few extra minutes before you leave the house to give yourself a once-over. A quick stop in the company's restroom, if a stop is convenient, prior

to going in to meet your new prospective employer, is always prudent for a last-minute check. (We can't stress enough how important the first impression is in this situation. Once you've made it, it's with that person forever.)

Remember that clothing is one of the ways we communicate nonverbally. Two people meeting for the first time have a conversation of sorts just by seeing what the other is wearing. And these "clothing conversations" can be formal or casual. Job interviews are almost always formal. Some corporate cultures allow a relaxed interview atmosphere, but, as mentioned earlier, it's always better to play it safe and dress conservatively.

A final piece of advice about job interviewing fashion. Whether you're dressing casually or formally, you should always wear one item: a watch. This not only helps you be on time, but it also sends an important message to the interviewer. It says that you are organized and are aware of where you need to be and when you need to be there. People who dress casually need to be on time as much as people who wear suits.

Employers are looking for somebody who will fit in, who can be part of their "team." So, in general, the interview is not the moment to make a fashion statement. You can liven up your look a little after you've been on the job a while, but pay attention to how people are dressed when you're there for the interview. You may find that the compa-

ny isn't the right fit for you (and after all, you're interviewing them as well). If how people dress is too buttoned-down or too free-form for you, the company may be too buttoned-down or too free-form a place for you to work.

... You're on a Date

A friend told us the story of a date she once had. She met on a blind date at a restaurant near the financial district (he was an accountant). As she entered the restaurant, she saw several men waiting, all dressed in what looked like identical suits. One man, though, stood out. It wasn't his suit, but his shoes. Among this group of expensive suits, he was the only one wearing a bright new pair of Nikes. As fate would have it, he was her date. As fate would further have it, they eventually got married, but it took a lot of convincing for him to get her to go out on the second date. She just couldn't get that first look of him in a suit and sneakers out of her mind.

If first impressions are critical on job interviews, you can imagine what they're like on dates. Let's say you have a date after work and you want to wear something casual, but you don't want to look like a college student on the weekend. First, dress honestly. A magazine editor tells the story of interviewing the Hell's Angels. Rather than trying to fit in and wear big boots and black leather, he wore simple, casual

clothes. The interview went fine because he was comfortable. He was himself and what he wore reflected that.

It's no different on a date. If you're ill at ease in what you're wearing—whether your clothes say Wall Street banker and your personality says bike messenger, or your clothes say performance artist and your personality says professor— she'll know.

The single biggest rule about dressing for a date is to know what you look best in. Dressing up a little nicer than usual helps, and being fashionable is good. Not surprisingly, most women appreciate it if you look like you actually prepared a bit just to meet them. But, in the end, you have to feel good about yourself and know what looks best on you.

Just as you would at work, dress appropriately for your surroundings, which in this case is wherever you're going on this date. Baseball game? Izod shirt and jeans are just fine. But if you're going someplace nice, dress nicely. When attending a performance of "Carmen," leave the jeans and the khakis in the closet. Opt for a rayon shirt with a silk blend or cashmere jacket. If you want to be elegant, you can put a mock turtleneck under the jacket. You can also dress up the shirt you wore to work with a festive tie, something with color and pattern. But there are no magic colors or styles that are guaranteed always to charm: *You* have to supply the charm. One final tip, however. Whether going to a baseball game or to a fancy club, always bring a layering piece (sweat-

shirt, jacket, or sweater). Your date just might get cold, and now you can offer to comfort her!

By the way, the answers to the quiz at the start of the chapter are all false. But you know that now, don't you?

5

THE ALREADY
WELL STOCKED
CASUAL CLOSET

Learn that clothes are there to suit your life,
not to run it.
JOHN WEITZ

50% or more (of those surveyed) agree:

I primarily shop for replacements (59%).

Price is a key consideration in my apparel purchases (57%).

I like to shop (43%).

In business casual dressing, audience analysis means knowing whom you're dealing with so that what you're wearing matches the situation. But in deciding how to create a casual wardrobe, you need to conduct another analysis. Although the analysis is basic, for most people it's difficult: You have to be able to analyze yourself. You have to be able to realize what makes you comfortable, not just in a physical sense, but also in a fashion sense and, as importantly, in a mental sense.

What does this mean? It's easy to know what clothes make you comfortable physically: that ancient leather jacket, the oversized T-shirt, the jeans you've had since college (and miraculously still fit). But what's more difficult to know is the type of business casual wear that makes you comfortable. If you were to try on a variety of jacket styles, tie patterns, and shoes, your level of physical comfort would probably be about the same. But when you look in the mirror, you may not be sure whether you look better (and hence feel better about yourself) wearing a corduroy jacket or a tweed blazer, a pair of khakis or dark jeans, loafers or boots.

Think back to the Image Ink Blot test you took a few chapters back, which listed nine occupations. The test would have been made much tougher if we had added an eleventh: yours. This is because it's easy for us to picture how other people look when they go to work. After all, we see them everyday at the office, on the commute, and at meetings. And this leads us to think that we should look a certain way also. Yes, we all need to fit in to a certain extent (we are, after all, in the same army), but we also need to stand our own fashion ground to the extent that we are not trying to be someone we're not.

For all we have said and will say about fitting what you wear to where you are, another fit is just as important: fitting what you wear to *who* you are.

The Leather Lawyer

We are reminded of a sports lawyer attending a meeting to sign a free agent baseball player as a client. He was told beforehand that the meeting would be casual. At that point he had to define "casual" and how he fit into it. Unfortunately, he chose to dress in a very flashy leather jacket style, one that he thought would match his rich, potential client.

As you've probably already guessed, he showed up feeling very uncomfortable with how he looked, physically and mentally. Because of this, his would-be client was equally uncomfortable. Just as important, the player didn't want a lawyer who dressed in leather. He wanted someone who projected the image of knowing the law. The lawyer never got his business because he never got the chance to show who he really was. People in business have a need and a right to know who they'll be dealing with. There's nothing wrong with a lawyer who wears a leather jacket, but who can place faith in a lawyer who wears leather just to be someone he's not?

Hence the rule of thumb: Since you're wearing the clothes, you need to be comfortable in them. If you feel foolish in something, don't wear it because someone else convinces you that it's correct or that it's the "right" image. How you feel comes through loud and clear, and that message is much louder and clearer than any statement you make with your wardrobe.

Your Personal Style

Even if you think of yourself as fashion brain-dead, you actually have some sense of style, even if you're not aware of

it: You have an image of yourself. You don't need a personality test or a list of traits to tell you what to do. But you can ask yourself a couple of questions to help define your image:

✔ Are you traditional or contemporary?

✔ Do you want to be noticed or do you want to blend in?

There aren't right or wrong answers to those questions. Even if you've never asked them of yourself out loud before, you've already answered them, not just in how you dress, but in you how you are, how you work with colleagues, how you are in the world.

Like people, companies are either traditional or contemporary, and if you had to give those styles a color, you'd say either navy or black. With navy (traditional) come other colors like tan and white and pastels, and fabrics like oxford cloth, twills, herringbone, and prints with small, tight patterns. With black (contemporary) come other colors like grays and greens (dark) and splashes of bright colors, and fabrics with texture, with multicolored weaves, prints with large repeating patterns, linens, and silks. So, whichever style you find fits you, you need to decide how much you want to be noticed for your clothing—and that decision determines how bright and how bold you want your choices to be.

This seems to make sense on paper, but maybe you're not sure what to make of it in practice. If that's so, look at what you already wear. If that doesn't help, go to the store. Go not to buy, but just to look and maybe to try some things on. See what feels comfortable and what makes your skin crawl. The chances are that you'll find you knew where you fit all along, even if you didn't have the words to describe it. But don't be surprised if you're a cross-over dresser. Many people live navy lives in daytime, and black lives at nighttime.

Now you're ready to go shopping for your new casual business wardrobe. But before you go out, let's go in—into your closet. You probably already have some of the elements of that new look.

Your New Old Clothes

Before going out and spending money on a new wardrobe, go through all your closets and drawers to see what you can use to create your new casual look. Many of the best fashion designers have said that when it comes to getting started with a new fashion concept, they first venture into the closet. You will likely find a shirt or a pair of pants or even a jacket that you bought and somehow forgot about.

You'll be surprised what you might find in your own closets, drawers, and storage spaces. You may have banished a shirt to the back of the closet because it was out of fashion, but, upon discovering it years later, you realize that the fashion is now back in. (Fashion is a fairly cyclical phenomenon:

If something is "out" today, you can bet it will be "in" again in a few years.) Ralph Lauren once said that fashion is not what is new, rather what you decide to bring back.

Or maybe your taste has changed. Remember, if having a business casual wardrobe is new to you, perhaps you dismissed clothes in your past because there wasn't any appropriate place to wear them.

You may have changed physically as well. While we typically tend to gain weight as we get older, many people's weight goes up and down like a streetcar in San Francisco. Therefore you may now be able to fit into something that you put away for storage a long time ago.

The point is that you should look through every storage space you have to see if you have clothes or accessories that may be helpful to you in creating the new casual you. Once you've done that, you should separate all the items into categories and take stock of what you have. How many jackets do you own? How many shirts? Pants? Shoes? Socks? Belts? Sweaters? You probably won't have enough to create a wardrobe, but you will see how much you already own.

Once you have everything out of the closets and drawers, you have to try them on. This is when things can get a little painful. There's nothing worse than finding an old pair of khakis that you loved, trying them on, and finding that they are not what they once were. (Actually, you're probably the one who's changed but it's much easier to blame it on the

pants.) If you think that there's no chance of your ever getting into a piece of clothing, dispose of it. Whether you give it to a younger relative, Goodwill, or back to whoever gave it to you, just make sure you clear it out of the house so that you have space to organize your new purchases.

Creating Your Business Casual Look

And what should those purchases be? To make the decisions easier for you, we've divided the myriad casual styles into degrees. You'll find our top ten lists in each category.

✔ Listed in the first are the essentials for what we'll call a *dress-down* informal casual business look.

✔ In the second are the basic elements for a more *conservative casual* business wardrobe.

✔ In the third are the elements for a more *dress-up* formal casual business look.

Again, as you go through these lists (and your closet), think about what you'd feel comfortable wearing and what you see your colleagues wearing at work. Remember also that these are the basics—the items or types of items you start with—not an exhaustive list of everything you can wear.

The Top Ten List for a Dress-Down Casual Business Look

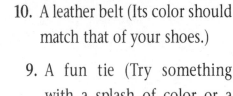

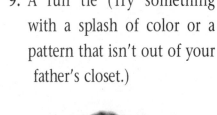

10. A leather belt (Its color should match that of your shoes.)

9. A fun tie (Try something with a splash of color or a pattern that isn't out of your father's closet.)

8. A blazer (If you only have one, navy is a good place to start. A neutral color is also good. Wool is the right material, but be sure to take into account the weight with the season.)

7. A crewneck sweater (Cotton should be your first choice for all year round. Wool works, too, as a classy second choice.)

6. Loafers (The usual colors—black, brown, or cordovan—are fine. Bucks and saddleshoes are also good choices, but not a first choice. Deck shoes often work, as do clean canvas sneakers.)

5. A blue denim shirt (This can be worn with or without a tie. Blue chambray in a point or button-down collar is equal to the task.)

4. A banded collar shirt in white oxford or chambray blue.

3. Blue jeans. (These are neither the same jeans you wear to play flag football on the weekend, nor tight jeans, even if you've got the physique to wear them. Classic looking stone washed jeans are at their most elegant with a blazer, polo, or oxford shirt with Bass Weejun penny loafers.

2. Khakis (If you own only one pair of slacks, make them khakis.)

1. An Izod-style shirt or sport shirt (Go for muted solid colors, but nothing too loud, and no slogans.)

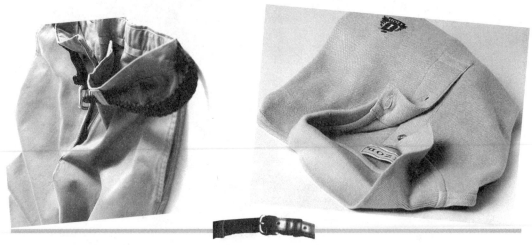

The Top Ten List for a More Formal Business Casual Look

What if you want to be casual, but not too casual? The following items are categorized as the formal business casual.

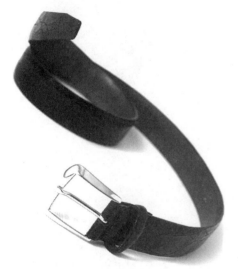

10. A leather belt (It still has to match the shoes.)

9. Shoes (These may be loafers, but with tassels, or just go with a pair of lace-ups.)

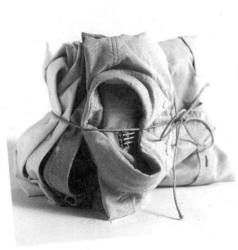

8. Shirts (Try chambray, and white or pastel oxford 100% cotton buttoned-down or spread collar.)

7. A cardigan sweater

6. A repp tie or knit tie

5. Khakis

4. Argyle or dark socks

3. The blazer (You get less choice here: navy. Be sure it's natural fiber. A textured weave will work well, too.)

2. A woven buttoned-down shirt (A white, blue, or subtle pattern is suitable.)

1. Gray or tan color wool slacks (As always, make sure they're pressed. *Note:* Gray slacks in any fabric other than wool should be left in the closet.)

The Top Ten List for a More Dress-Up Business Casual Look

10. A leather belt (It still has to match the shoes.)

9. Shoes (Leather lace-ups or loafers with tassels will do.)

8. Shirts (Again, look for chambray, and white or pastel 100% cotton oxford buttoned-down.)

7. A cashmere sweater

6. A silk tie

5. Dressy slacks with a slight pattern

4. Dark socks

3. Blazer (Again, select navy or other dark color, midweight wool. Again, be sure it's of natural fiber.)

2. A woven buttoned-down shirt (White, blue, or subtle pattern goes well.)

1. Gray or other neutral color slacks (Again, make sure they're pressed.)

You'll notice that the differences among the three lists are largely a matter of degree: how far away you move from traditional business wear and how much flair you toss in with what you wear. You'll also notice that a sports jacket or a blazer of some sort is an absolute essential, but there's a lot of variation in what goes on underneath the jacket. You always want a tie and a pair of leather shoes in the closet for when you might need them, even if you don't wear them every day. Keep in mind, however, that other matters can factor into what you wear and when you wear it. An example is the season. Although a knit shirt may be ideal for the casual look you are seeking to portray, that selection may not work in the middle of January in Minneapolis where it's 25 degrees below zero. Perhaps a Gant longsleeve rugby shirt would do the trick.

A Starting Point

But how do you get to this point? It's one thing to give you top ten lists, but the items on the lists don't just materialize in your closet. Obviously you have to go out and buy them. But where to start? If you go to the store and pick out the ten items, there's no guarantee that they'll go together.

The best way to begin is to choose one item on the list. Let's say you want to start with the blazer. (Jackets are always a good starting point since they usually cost the most.) Go to a local clothier and give yourself plenty of time (this is casual wear, after all). See what appeals to you. Try on many styles, colors, and cuts. Ask salespersons what they think. (Usually at finer stores they'll be honest with you; they won't sell you what you don't need.). Better yet, bring along a spouse or a friend. Ultimately, however, the choice must be yours. Consider each jacket you try on. Does it look like you? Does it feel physically comfortable? Does it project an image that is appropriate to your job and who you are?

Once you've decided on a jacket, use that as a starting point to complete the rest of the top ten list. If you went with a navy blazer, which pants and shoes look good with it? If you decided on the navy blazer, which sweaters and ties match? (Don't worry. The answers to these questions are in an upcoming chapter. But the good news is that almost anything in any color will go well with a navy blazer and khakis.)

Once you have the first building block in your new fashion structure, the rest comes relatively easily since you have a point of reference. As you add each item, always take your time and always make sure that it is something that you would wear anyway, with or without the jacket.

How to Shop for the Casual Look

You're probably going to have to shop in a new way. Traditionally, men buy a shirt if they need a shirt, a pair of pants if they need pants, and so on. Now, however, you want to buy a shirt that goes with a pair of pants and a jacket (maybe pants and a jacket you already have). You want your clothes to work together, so that, out of a couple of shirts, a couple of pairs of slacks, a jacket, and a sweater, you can match different colors and different degrees of dressiness. Then you've got a couple of weeks worth of outfits to wear to work.

Intelligent, coordinated purchasing is only one shopping strategy. Another is based on common sense but it is something that all savvy casual shoppers do: Before going out to the store, make a list.

This has a few good side effects. Obviously the first is that you won't forget what you came to buy. How often have you gone to the store to get, say, three things, and once you're there, you can remember only the first two? By writing down what you need, you avoid having to go back to the store (which for some men is a fate worse than death). Another benefit is that it helps you think. Creating lists is basically brainstorming. By writing out your ideas, you might stumble on a fashion need that would otherwise have been overlooked. Finally, if money is a problem, a list forces you to stick to just a few items and saves you from impulse buying.

Where to Shop for the Casual Look

There is also the question of where to shop for business casual wear. Chances are that your local department store

(Macy's, May Co., Belks, Dillards, etc.), where you might buy some of your formal wear, is also one of the best outlets for casual wear. Certain speciality stores such as The Gap or Banana Republic are equally adept at creating a new casual you.

In fact, a growing number of retail stores now cater to the man who wants to dress casually. These stores are becoming increasingly popular, reflecting the fact that many more people today are looking for such clothes.

If you need your new casual clothes yesterday, obviously you can't wait—but keep your eye out for frequent sales. One last money-saving tip: When *adding* to your casual wardrobe, usually the best time to shop for seasonal casual clothes is at the end of the season. For example, if you're looking for fall and winter clothing (jackets, sweaters, etc.), the best time to hit the stores is in late January. If you want good deals on spring and summer clothes (linens, white shirts), then August is usually the best time. Be aware, though, that we are not the only ones giving this advice. The stores are flooded with people looking for the same items; so don't be too disappointed if what you're looking for is sold out.

If you really care about clothes, then be ready when the new lines are launched. You may pay regular prices, but you ensure getting your size and color. After all, this is an investment. Choosing, rather than settling, protects your investment.

The Casual Closet

Dressing is a matter of mixing and matching. One day you wear the banded collar shirt buttoned up to the neck with a jacket over it. The next day underneath that jacket you have your shirt opened at the neck with a T-shirt underneath. Some days a sweater replaces the jacket, and other days you wear the sweater under the jacket. We'll have more to say about mixing later. For now, however, let's go back to your closet. In the casual closet you're going to have two sides. One side contains all the casual items that are appropriate to wear to work. On the other side are all the clothes that make you feel physically comfortable but will never be a welcome sight at the office. It's important to make the distinction between the two sides of the closet.

And know this: The route between the two sides of the casual closet is one-way. Shirts, jackets, and pants eventually travel from the appropriate side to the not appropriate side. But once they're there, they stay there. Casual clothes, once retired, should stay retired. Comebacks are nice for politicians and basketball players (sometimes), but not for clothes.

Business Casual Don'ts

Making an inappropriate clothing item appropriate is what we might call a "business casual don't." Some business casual don'ts are matters of fashion: looks that have come and gone, looks that haven't come in the first place. Other casual dress don'ts are matters of context: looks that work somewhere, but not at work.

Other business casual don'ts include:

✔ *Polyester.* Some new blends work, and some man-made fabrics work for certain items. In general, though, go natural with your choice of fabrics. The primary exception is the new and very popular wrinkle-free blends that have a blend of cotton and polyester but are crisp and clean. New technology also offers wrinkle-free cotton options. These work well, but are just short of the elegance of true natural cotton.

✔ *Jewelry.* No, this isn't an absolute, but keep it minimal and keep it simple, whether it's the ring you wear around your finger or through your ear.

Other dont's follow.

T-shirts or sweatshirts with messages on them. Too often when you think it's funny, your coworkers think it's silly, juvenile, sexist, etc. It's always best to make your statement with your pencil, not your stencil.

Short-sleeved buttoned shirts, unless you're out to recreate that 1950s industrial engineer look or work in a rural humid climate.

Skin (yours). Don't show it. That means socks long enough to cover your leg when you sit down or cross your legs. It also means no tank tops or sleeveless T's.

Shorts or cutoffs, unless you work for a cybersurfing boss who wears them. But don't be the first person to wear shorts to the office .

Professional sports jerseys. Save them for the weekend.

Clothes that don't fit. For example, the street look where pants are so long that they drag on the ground.

Tight jeans. Even if you've worked hard on that body, the office is not the right place to show it.

Open collar with a tie, makes you look too hassled.

Anything frayed or dirty.

If you have any of these items move them to the right side of the closet, for weekend wear.

Some other business casual dont's are obvious but are often overlooked. Casual does not mean sloppy. That means no wrinkles and no holes. No fraying collars and no distressed jeans. If you're wearing shoes that were meant to be polished, they should be polished. Pants should be pressed. (Even jeans should be ironed, but without center creases. Who would do that anyway?) And, of course, nothing should be dirty. Remember again that there is no substitute for soap and water. Business casual starts with good grooming.

6

THE ABCs
OF BUSINESS
CASUAL WEAR

What sets a man apart from animals
is his ability to accessorize.
SPY MAGAZINE

It's alright to let yourself go as long as
you can let yourself back.
MICK JAGGER

Top 10 reasons for choosing a store for men's apparel purchases

1. Good selection (25.4%)
2. The best value (23.6%)
3. You like the store (11.1%)
4. Convenient location (9.3%)
5. It's easy to shop there (9.2%)
6. Best size fit (9.0%)
7. It carries name brands (4.1%)]
8. It accepts credit cards (3.9%)
9. Good service (3.8%)
10. Good sale prices (0.1%)

More than anything, this chapter is a list. Now that you have the top ten types of items you need for the various business casual wardrobes, you can make your actual choices from the longer lists in this chapter. While you might not be familiar with each term (houndstooth, cordovan, etc.), you'll be able to ask specific questions of the sales clerks.

Don't feel overwhelmed by the lists, which just set out the elements of style, all the different pieces that go into making a business casual wardrobe. You don't need everything on the list, and, depending on where you work, you won't *want* everything on the list. But wherever you work, the lists give you the raw materials. (In Chapter 7 we'll show you how to fit the various elements into complete outfits.)

Jackets

Your jacket, the logical place to start your casual wardrobe, is usually also the first apparel item people see when they meet you. (Your face will be noticed first, followed by the overall impression created by your jacket and, more importantly, your shirt.) Here are the basic types of jacket you should consider:

✔ Navy blazer (wool), single-breasted with gold buttons; flannel in winter, worsted in spring and summer (*Note:* Worsted is acceptable 12 months per year)

✔ Navy blazer, double-breasted (6 buttons); flannel in winter, worsted in spring and summer

✔ Camel blazer; can be cashmere, but also wool for winter; khaki linen in summer; "solid" pattern jacket; or a subtle tweed, herringbone, or houndstooth

Your jacket—the first thing people notice about your clothes

✔ Cotton twill; lightly washed (distressed), then pressed; neutral colors

✔ Three-button jacket (optional), navy or black

✔ Four-button jacket (a younger look), black or dark gray (natural tan in summer)

Pants

Pants are important not only in how they work with the rest of your casual ensemble, but also in how they feel. A pair of casual pants should be comfortable, but not everyone is built the same. A fabric or cut that's comfortable for one person may be agony for someone else. And don't forget that comfort also means how you look, not just how you feel. When in doubt, buy a size larger.

The types of business casual pants include:

✔ Khaki pants: khaki, tan, olive, oyster, chino, tan, tan, and more tan

✔ Navy pants: cotton twill

✔ Gray flannel wool slack (for winter)

Pants must look good and feel good on you

✔ Gray worsted wool slack (for summer)

✔ Jeans (always stone washed, always pressed, but not creased)

✔ Wide-wale corduroys (for winter)

✔ Navy, brown, or black slacks or shades of tan and green in wool gabardine

✔ Pants in textured fabrics (but they must look solid)

✔ Cuffs and pleats (We love them! But note that nonpleated twills are looking good as an alternative.)

Shirts

While the jacket is the first thing people notice about you, your shirt defines who you are more than any other item. You are seen without a jacket and without a tie from time to time, but you always keep your shirt on. (We know that you should probably also keep your pants on as well, but, if you think about it, you're often seen sitting at

Your shirt says who you are

your desk or at a conference table. No one sees the pants you're wearing, but your shirt is always in view.)

As with pants (and anything, really), style and comfort should go hand in hand. A tight collar might look nice to everyone else, but what's the use of looking good if you're constantly passing out due to a lack of oxygen? So, be sure to buy the correct neck size.

With that in mind, here is a list of casual shirt types:

✔ White buttoned-down shirt

✔ Woven shirts (blue, white, and pink)

✔ Turtleneck/mock turtleneck

✔ Pique polo with collar

✔ Sport shirts/golf shirts

✔ T-shirt, crewneck (not V)

✔ Formal sport shirt, buttoned all the way up with no tie

✔ Collarless (banded collar) shirt

✔ Ginghams, plaids, and stripes (classics)

✔ Chambray (especially in blue)

✔ Oxford-style shirt (white, blue, or pink)

✔ Blue denim shirt (point collar, button-down collar, or banded collar)

✔ Chambray (point collar, button-down collar, or banded collar)

✔ Cotton twills (all colors)

✔ Rayon or collared sport shirt

As for logo shirts—*leave 'em at home!*

The rule of thumb for sleeves: Long sleeve sport shirts work all year round, and short sleeve sport shirts work for spring and summer.

Sweaters

A good sweater is sometimes an accessory and sometimes a necessity. Sweaters become a casual dress option more often in the winter as a matter of practicality. A sweater can give you a more relaxed look. Depending on the fabric and style, it can make you look younger or more mature. It can also add color to your wardrobe. The first rule: classic, classic, classic. Additional sweater suggestions include:

✔ Cardigan, neutrals or earth tones, black, navy, green, 100% cotton

✔ V-neck sweater, knit wool, with an elastic waist, any color

✔ Knit collar sweater, preferably with cable front

✔ Sweatshirt (some places)

✔ Vest, pull-over or button front, in solids or patterns

The right sweater can make you look relaxed, younger—or older

✔ Short- or long-sleeved cashmere polo sweater in black or neutral color

✔ Mock or turtleneck sweater

✔ Crewneck in cotton, any color (this is the classic)

Remember: A sweater is a wonderful casual substitute for a jacket.

Shoes

Comfort is especially important when it comes to shoes, particularly if you're on your feet for most of the day. While it probably feels most comfortable to wear a pair of high tops or sandals to the office, the company dress code more than likely frowns on them.

Shoes are also important in that the wrong pair of shoes can turn a casual look into an inappropriate look. People notice what's on your feet. So be sure they don't notice for all the wrong reasons.

Our list of casual shoes includes:

✔ Classic loafer [Cordovan (wine) is always a smart choice]

✔ Dress lace-up, nonglossy buff

✔ Boots, but be careful. (Rugged boots are in style for winter and inclement weather. Cowboys—stay home.)

Get the shoes right—don't get noticed for the wrong reason

✔ Deck shoes

✔ Bass Weejun penny loafers

✔ Tassel loafer

✔ Suede (nubuck) shoes, loafer or lace-up.

✔ Saddle shoes and bucks (forever a classic)

Another hint for shoes: match your shoes with your belt (black shoes–black belt, brown shoes–brown belt).

Socks

A nice pair of socks can be an effective accessory to what you're wearing. The main differences between casual socks and formal socks are the thickness and the color. Socks in business casual wear tend to be thicker and hence more comfortable. Think about this upfront when trying on shoes in the store. Many people forget to consider the thickness of the sock they will be wearing. The last thing you want is a pair of new shoes that fit too tightly.

Sometimes red socks work

You can also get away from the standard black, blue, and brown of the socks you'd wear with a suit. Sometimes a pair of pink or yellow socks looks good and adds character to your look. (As always, avoid any socks that are tattered or too loud.)

A few suggestions:

✔ Blacks, grays, and tans

✔ Argyles

✔ Patterned socks, in muted colors

Tips on Socks

1. Never arrive at work without wearing socks unless the boss does as well!

2. Match your socks to your pants

Suits

We usually associate suits with formal business wear, but a few types can be considered casual. Try a suit with a soft shape and a natural fit. Also, look at suits made out of soft, textured fabrics. The stuffy pinstripe was not the only suit ever created. Some suits can look very casual. Remember to button the shirt to the neck.

Some suits can be casual

These lists are by no means complete, but they give you choices to start with. From these lists, you should be able to establish a firm casual fashion foundation, which, with mixing and matching, should be relatively inexpensive. You can get a lot of mileage out of a relatively small number of items. But again remember, good quality often costs more. And when buying classic styles, they will remain classics for a lifetime.

At the end of the day, it's all how you put it together, which leads us to the next chapter.

7

PUTTING IT
ALL TOGETHER

The well dressed man never stands out in a
crowd; his elegance sets him apart.
OSCAR DE LA RENTA

All dressed up and nowhere to go.
WILLIAM ALLEN WHITE

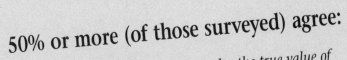

50% or more (of those surveyed) agree:

I am confident in my ability to judge the true value of clothing (73%).

I shop primarily for fashion (52%).

Y ou've gone on a casual shopping spree, and you now have all the basic clothes identified in the last several chapters. While you may have been mixing and matching in your mind while shopping, now you're really going to do something with your selections. In this chapter we'll lead you through a variety of combinations, from simple to complex. The key is versatility!

Mixing and matching entails an almost infinite number of possibilities. A college professor we know approaches it mathematically. He has a certain number of shirts, ties, jackets, and pants. He calculates how many classes he has and the number of clothing combinations available. He then charts what he'll wear for the entire semester (sort of a clothing syllabus). While this is a bit extreme (and a little neurotic), it shows the number of possibilities that are available.

If you had to pick a single casual classic, it would be a white buttoned-down shirt with a pair of khakis and cordovan loafers. From that simple beginning, all sorts of combinations are possible.

A lively combination of shirt, tie, and pants

Shirts

Begin with the traditional button-down shirt and tie, but don't stop there. Liven up that basic combination with a tie that has some color or a pattern. You don't have to wear a blazer; try a vest or patterned sport coat. You can also take that same shirt and tie combination and pull a crew- or V-neck sweater over it.

A more elegant, but casual look

For a more elegant casual look, keep the jacket, but replace the buttoned-down shirt with a turtleneck. You can also achieve a certain contemporary elegance with a banded collar shirt buttoned up to the top. Or try a shirt in a more elegant fabric, such as linen or rayon, buttoned up, with a jacket but no tie.

For a more casual look, try an Izod pique golf shirt instead of the turtleneck. This classic knit wonder works in almost any color with khakis and penny loafers. For something casual in a different direction, bring back the buttoned-down shirt—a woven shirt this time—leave the top two buttons open, and wear a T-shirt underneath (something in a muted color, either the same as the top shirt or in a complementary

A touch of color in the shirt

color). The chambray and the denim share some of the casual terrain, but the chambray is a little dressier, with or without a tie.

You can slip colors in with the shirt. Remember that, as a rule, you don't want more than three colors at one time, and usually you don't want more than one stand-out color. (We'll be going into more detail about colors and color combinations in Chapter 8.)

Jackets

You have a lot of options, but always stick to natural fibers. You could actually wear a suit. You won't wear this every day, but look for something with a relaxed, natural fit and made of a material with character to it—something with a little texture, something in a soft fabric. You might find yourself looking at a wool-silk blend, for example, or something linen or cotton (for the summer months).

Of course, the jacket spectrum has two extremes. From the basic to the basically outrageous, there are many choices in jackets. You can go for just about anything from a traditional navy blazer (another of those items that may not cause a stir at the office, but one you can't go wrong with) to something in a subtle solid texture. You'll find:

✔ Jackets with three buttons and four (a younger, contemporary style).

✔ Camel jackets (they don't have to be cashmere; you'll find them in linen or cotton, too).

✔ Jackets in muted darker colors, and sometimes washed cotton in neutral colorations.

Look for fabrics with pattern and texture: an unsolid solid, herringbone, or houndstooth. The Italian designers have worked miracles in this area.

Don't bother taking one piece of traditional advice, which is to match the jacket to the pants. That's a legacy of the ancient regime, the time of the suits, when jackets and pants matched precisely. Today, a patterned jacket with pants of a solid color, or a jacket and pants each having a different shade of the same color, or something like a linen jacket over a pair of blue jeans—they can all work at the office these days. They call them sport coats for a reason!

Sweaters

In business casual wear, you can think of the sweater as an alternate form of jacket. Start with a cardigan, which you can wear just as if it were a jacket. (Just don't get too dressy underneath.) You can put a crewneck sweater over a shirt and tie, you can drop the tie and open the top button of your shirt, or you can go more informal and just wear the crewneck. Alternatively, you can choose a V-neck wool sweater in

A sweater can replace the jacket

a neutral color, like navy or gray, with a T-shirt underneath. (Do we need to mention again that T-shirt does not mean outrageous colors, anything with words or pictures, or a V-neck?) The V-neck sweater can also be topped off by a jacket, but you want something relaxed, a looser fit than the standard suit coat. You need room to ensure that the look is not form fitting. The sweater really is the best alternative to a jacket, and still is casual and fashionably correct.

Pants

Now back to the khakis. To go with them you can select a sport coat for wear over the white shirt. You can also pair up a blue denim shirt and a fun tie (meaning something with a splash of color or an interesting pattern), with or without a jacket.

The types of pants you select collectively reflect on your personality, as well as your sense of the style of the day. Corduroys and wide-wales work nicely with a sweater (in winter). If the office rules say jeans are acceptable, you have another element to work with, and you can achieve very elegant (chic) looks with jeans. Try, for example, a worsted wool sport coat for one direction, or something in a solid textured wool for another. Sweaters, of course, go well with jeans, and include vests in your sweater line-up. Then, bottom off with a classic cordovan penny loafer.

Socks

One school of thought says that your socks should match your pants, but there's more than one school of fashion thought out there. White socks, for example, work if you're going for a certain style of casual (the khaki and loafer look). Pastels look great with jeans. And you can use argyles to add an element of color and pattern. Remember two things about socks: First, when you're standing up or walking around, nobody's going to see your socks unless your pants don't fit. Second, be careful and judicious. Very often, when people size you up, after your face they look at your shoes. Shoes are said to be the fashion window to your sole (soul). So, when it comes to socks, nothing too bright or too wild.

Shoes

Shoes follow rather than lead, both in style and color. Since you're dressing more casually from the ankles up, you don't want to finish the look with a contrasting pair of fancy shoes, such as Italian loafers, unless you are in black or black contemporary. If you want something more casual, try a pair of conventional loafers. If you need to be on the dressy side, you can choose tassel loafers or a pair of lace-up shoes. Tradition has dictated black shoes with any dark outfit, and brown shoes with something in the browns. While you can generally rest assured with black, there's a movement toward

more brown with anything dark. So if you're not sure, black is your safest choice.

If the look *du jour* includes jeans, you might consider a range of shoes, from boots (not motorcycle boots) to penny loafers to deck shoes (if they work in your office). And you can also try a pair of nubuck suede shoes, brown or black.

Belts

There's not a lot to say about belts beyond the need to match the belt with the shoes (black shoes, black belt and brown shoes, brown belt). Buckles should be simple and not too big (no initials or diamond studs).

Again, these are only a few possibilities for putting together the various pieces of your casual fashion puzzle. Luckily, unlike a jigsaw puzzle, there are many correct answers. Find out what works best for you by experimenting. Take time at home to try combinations that you hadn't considered before. You never know what you might stumble on. After all, you weren't born yesterday. You have experience and a sense of style already.

To put together the pieces of the fashion puzzle, you need to be familiar with the characteristics of your clothes. A most important characteristic is color, which we discuss in the next chapter.

8

SOME COLORS JUST DON'T LOOK GOOD

It's better to have poor taste than no taste at all.
UNKNOWN

50% or more (of those surveyed) agree:

Finding a bargain is not as important as finding the right quality (57%).

T he first rule about color is that there isn't any rule. Like everything else about business casual, you start by noticing what types and brightnesses of color people in your corporate culture are wearing. In some offices, brightly colored Hawaiian shirts or neon-striped Spandex biking shorts are the order of the day, and, if you happen to work in such an office, the sky's the limit on colors.

For the rest of us, there may not be rules, but there are guidelines. One of them is not to use color to make a specific statement, such as, I will put on a color today that makes me look powerful and sexy. It doesn't work like that. People perceive colors differently. Just as tastes differ, so do reactions to colors. If we have learned one lesson from all our years in the clothing industry, it's that people's tastes in colors obey no universal rules. While a vast majority of people might think that purple represents royalty, others are turned off by it completely. And if you dress all in black thinking that you've cornered the market in hip, you may look too sophisticated for the office. So, when in doubt, stay neutral.

Also consider that people react just as much to the combination of colors as they do to any one color. While there might be no across-the-board reaction to an individual color, you can bet the house that, if you walk into the office on Monday wearing a black jacket over an orange shirt, you'll hear more than one wisecrack about Halloween and perhaps become an instant object of ridicule. But, nevertheless, black on black is now preceived as chic.

Which Colors Work?

Here's another guideline. You just can't go wrong with some colors, and those colors are your building blocks. Some colors you can introduce here and there, and some colors almost never work at work.

So, let's open the employee palette.

As you might guess, the safest colors are the most neutral ones: black, navy, gray, dark green, and khaki. Neutral

Some colors are building blocks—you can't go wrong with them

col-
ors work precisely because they are neutral. They don't make
a statement for you or against you; they just get you in the
door. And for most men, muted colors and dark colors go
over better than bright colors and multicolored fabrics. Save
the bright color for an accent, a splash (in a tie, for example).

Speaking of ties and color, the power tie as a fashion
statement has probably taken a place next to the leisure suit,
even though red does signify power to many.

Black still says contemporary. You can dress up or down by the type of black you wear, as in a silk or rayon shirt or a T-shirt. Khakis and a white shirt offer one sort of classic casual look, and a navy blazer with navy pants and a lively tie offer, another. Charcoal gray, light gray, and browns are all good colors. All of them are perfect with cordovan loafers.

Blue shirts and white shirts work best. You can throw in stripes as well, but most men feel more comfortable with no more than three different colors at any one time. Again, the cordovan loafers work extremely well. If you're wearing patterned clothing—a striped shirt and a herringbone jacket—make sure the patterns work together. You don't want lines running one way below the waist and another way above it. You also don't want your tie angling against your shirt and jacket.

Color Crazy

Don't make yourself crazy about colors, but at the same time don't be afraid to use them. You probably have a favorite color or two, and they are probably colors that look good on you. Be careful to choose the appropriate range of that color. Go easy on the royal blue, for instance, even if you do have baby blue eyes. Your favorite colors are your favorites because they are pleasing to your eyes, and there's no reason that you should always stay in the neutral range of colors.

Adding colors to your look is like adding paints to a canvas

Unless you do something outrageous, the colors you wear do not reshape your personality in other people's eyes. Even though color conveys meaning, it doesn't evoke a Pavlovian response. As an extreme example, if you wear a purple coat, people don't bow down and kiss your ring. Regard adding colors to your look as you would adding paint to a canvas. Your neutral base, say khaki, is the canvas. Once established, pastels, bright reds, royals, etc. all work because the khaki (canvas) base allows for such additions.

A Few Larger Ideas

There are some general associations between certain colors and a sense of style, as well as between certain colors and economic class. But these have been watered down so much as to be almost meaningless (as our Image Ink Blot test proved).

Nevertheless, to simplify these associations, go back to our division of all style into traditional and contemporary, which we can loosely associate with navy and black. With navy, we include tans and white. With black, we include grays, greens, and tans. (Pastels are traditional colors, but they are generally associated with old money, the leisure class.)

For those with firm beliefs that colors can indeed send messages, here are a couple of general rules. Any dark colors send a message of power and competency; light colors can make you seem more approachable, more friendly. For example, you might choose darks if, for reasons of age and experience, you're concerned about not being taken seriously. On the other hand, if people think you come on a little too strong or aggressively, light colors might take the edge off. Dark colors in a relatively monochromatic mix also tend to make you look slimmer. White has a brightening effect, and a white shirt makes a man look alive (it's also a good backdrop for a tie with color).

In general, just remember to use color subtly. Usually you don't want to walk through the office door in a color or combination of colors that makes everyone's head turn. You want people to see you and say, "He looks nice"—not, "Wow, look at him!" And if you just *have* to have one rule, try this one: When in doubt, white on navy.

One of the best ways to incorporate color into your look is to select ties that are colorful but tasteful. This leads us to the next chapter.

9

THE TIES
THAT BIND

Hast thou clothed his neck with thunder?

Job 39:19, "Psalms"

Thy neck is a tower of ivory.

Isaiah 7:4, "Song of Solomon"

Top 10 things most men dislike about shopping for apparel

1. The time it takes
2. Waiting on line
3. Trying on clothes
4. High prices
5. Pushy salespeople
6. The lack of size
7. The lack of service
8. Poor fit
9. Style selection
10. Color selection

A fter reading this chapter, you will be able to answer the nagging questions you've probably always had about ties:

How wide is the average tie?

Say, what's a club tie?

Honey, how should I store my knit ties?

Hmmm. How far down on my body should a tie hang?

Let's begin by saying that perhaps the most important fashion issue under attack in corporate casual dressing is the question of "to tie or not to tie." In meetings with executives in the neckware industry, we have suggested that they put their marketing dollars into promoting neckware as a major component of corporate casual dressing. The tie should be a wanted accessory in dressing down. However, clearly the elimination of this item is at the forefront of the casual revolution. As with most things in life, moderation equals motivation. Ties play a part only if you want them to. *They are not required.*

Dressing casually doesn't mean getting rid of your entire collection of ties. You might move some of your ties to the back of the closet, but there is certainly a place for ties in a business casual wardrobe. They just may not be the ties you're accustomed to wearing. After all, a tie is not only the lifeline to being dressed appropriately in a corporate casual environment, it is also the anti-statement of the corporate casual.

On the other hand, ties are the single safest place to add a pop of color or a touch of a complex pattern. You can be more expressive with a tie, and a good tie can add punch to your look. You probably wouldn't wear a pair of red pants or a paisley jacket to work, but either works just fine knotted at your neck. On the other hand, a bad tie can ruin an otherwise acceptable look. How many times have you seen someone wearing a truly awful tie?

Ties are a safe place to add a pop of color or pattern

After seeing them, you probably couldn't describe any other part of their wardrobe.

Tip: When choosing a tie to wear in the morning, have the tie pattern complement the jacket pattern.

What Types of Ties Are Available?

There are thousands of types of ties available. There are ties in solid colors, in psychedelic patterns, and in the shapes of animals and creatures (the old Ralph Marlin "fish ties" come to mind). Men have been known to wear ties connected to a battery that sport blinking light bulbs. Just remember: There is no substitute for good taste.

Novelty aside, there are several basic categories of ties:

✔ Repp ties (lined, conservative)

✔ Foulards (regular prints)

✔ Solids (knits and wools)

✔ Dots (the smaller the dots, the better)

✔ Club ties (with a specific pattern or insignia)

✔ Paisleys (always beautiful and multipurposed)

Any of these types are fine depending on the color, the patterns, and especially what else you happen to be wearing.

How Wide Should a Tie Be?

This is one of the most common questions asked about ties. Anyone who lived through the sixties, seventies, and eighties can tell you that the width of ties changed frequently. What was in one year was out the next. While it's fine to make a few fashion concessions to what's right for the time, it's also a good idea to have in stock some ties that never go out of style.

The average width of a tie over the years is approximately 3 inches at the widest part and usually about half that where the knot is made. This doesn't mean that you should take a tape measure to the clothing store; just don't go overboard on ties that are much wider or narrower than that. As far as length goes, the average is about 54 inches.

Since men come in different sizes, so do ties. If you're worried about buying a new tie and finding that it is too long or too short, take a tie with you shopping that you own, that ties easily, and that is the right length for you. Hold it next to the new tie to see if it measures up. You'll find that most ties come in one length. Some specialty stores carry inventory for very tall people.

All Tied Up

Tying a tie has always been a problem for men. The most common knot is the standard four-in-hand knot. There are also the Windsor knot (named after the Duke of Wind-

sor) and the more popular half-Windsor. Whichever you choose, have the knot take up the space between the collar ends at the top of the shirt.

Taking off the tie may seem simple, and it is. Yet many ties are ruined or damaged by men who yank off their ties and toss them to the floor at the end of the day. The best way to remove a tie is to simply reverse the steps you took in tying it. Try not to just pull down on the knot. This unties the tie, but it also stretches the fabric. Once you have the tie off, hang it up right away. Knit ties, however, should be rolled up and stored that way. If they hang on a rack, they can get stretched too much and lose their shape.

Here are some additional hints on tying ties:

✔ Be sure that the dimple in the knot is centered. If it's not, your whole look appears lopsided.

✔ Be sure the knot is tight enough to reach the top of the shirt. I know that loosening one's tie is a relief, but at least start the day with a crisp look, even in casual attire.

✔ Don't make the knot too big. This is a common mistake. If it does turn out too big, try a half-Windsor knot.

✔ When buying a tie, make sure it lies flat against your body. Otherwise its shape only gets worse.

✔ Avoid linen ties. They wear out too easily.

How to Tie a Tie

The Four-in-Hand

The Half-Windsor

✔ Be sure the end of the tie falls to the middle of your belt buckle.

✔ Most important, never wear a soiled tie!

In some circles, jackets and ties are required. Let's not let this requirement stand in the way of our choosing corporate casual. It works only if you want it to.

We've covered all the basics, right? Wrong. One major item remains. It is the item often overlooked and considered by many men to be a nonmaterial element when it comes to their wardrobe. This item is shoes. Don't be fooled or misled. Shoes are very important. The next chapter tells you why.

10

THE SOUL
OF SHOES

The shoe that fits one person pinches another.
CARL GUSTUV JUNG

Romans used shoes as an indication of the
social position of the wearer.

Once upon a time, two shoe salespersons were sent to a developing nation to search for opportunities. Upon arriving, they notice that no one was wearing shoes.

The first salesperson called the home office and said, "No one is wearing shoes. I'm leaving for home. There's no opportunity here."

The second salesperson called the home office and said, "No one is wearing shoes. Send more samples. Increase production. There's tremendous opportunity here. I'm extending my stay!"

Shoes have come a long way since the Egyptians developed sandals made of papyrus and palm leaves. As the fashion window to your soul, shoes send powerful messages about your sense of fashion, attention to detail, and meticulousness. The saying among fashion authorities is that, if you really want to know whether a man is well dressed, "look down." In fact, perhaps the worst fashion mistake you can

Shoes—the fashion window to your soul

make in putting together your new casual wardrobe is to transmit false messages about yourself—only because you tried to save money on shoes. Our advice is not to compromise on quality when it comes to shoes.

One more point: Recall from Chapter 4 that, when you're on the road, the important thing is not where you are, but whom you are seeing. When it comes to shoes, there is a caveat: Climate counts. If your meeting takes you to New York in the dead of winter, the brutal elements can literally tear your fine Italian loafers to shreds. Therefore, fashion correct footwear that delivers the correct level of performance is not only measured by cost, but also by the ability to meet your lifestyle needs.

The Anatomy of a Shoe

Well made shoes consist of four basic parts:

1. *Last.* This term refers to the shape of the shoe. The key measurements that go into the last are the length, width, and height of instep and arch.

2. *Skin.* Also referred to as the "upper," this is the material. We recommend leather, because it makes a shoe a shoe. It is the single largest factor that determines the price. It provides the wear, breathability, and high-quality appearance that is particular to a given pair of shoes.

3. *The sole and lining.* This is the bottom and inside of the shoe. Again, we recommend leather. However, if you're on your feet a lot, such as spending days at a time at trade shows, and need more shock absorption, consider some of the newer performance materials such as polyurethane, rubber, and KUA. We know of one executive whose back pain subsided dramatically when he switched to a more shock-absorbing shoe.

4. *Shank.* This is a piece of metal or plastic (steel is preferred) placed in the sole to reinforce and maintain the shoe's shape and structure. Primarily, it provides stability in the arch and heel area.

If the Shoe Fits ...

How should shoes fit? First, this should be comfortable! Nothing puts a damper on how you feel physically and emotionally like ill-fitting shoes. So, for comfort, remember a few rules of thumb when buying shoes. These rules are not absolute because every foot is as different as every type of shoe.

✔ Don't count on shoes stretching by up to one-half a size (even leather). If the shoes do not fit comfortably when you try them on, leave them at the store.

✔ Try on shoes with the type of sock you will be wearing with them.

✔ You should be able to wiggle your toes. A good rule to remember is that there should be about one-half inch of space between the tips of your toes and your shoes.

✔ The heel should fit snugly.

✔ Look for good arch support.

For the best look and good wear, consider two other guidelines:

✔ Consider leather first, not only because it allows your feet to breathe, but also because, from a value and quality standpoint, you will get more for your money.

✔ The first three colors of shoes you buy should be black, brown, and cordovan. If you're set on only two pairs, go with black and cordovan. Of course, this is very subjective, but in our experience, these colors are the most versatile.

From your foot's standpoint, the best time of the day to buy shoes is late in the day. Because feet swell, you'll get the most accurate size measurements *after* you've been up and about.

Taking Care of Shoes

Now let's discuss an aspect of shoes that most men ignore: maintenance. With proper care, shoes can last for many years. You'll be amazed how long the life of your shoes

can be extended by a little polish, a pair of shoe trees, and a periodic replacement of soles and heels.

Even though Chapter 12 discusses how to make your clothes look their best, because of the very important role shoes play in projecting your image, we thought it better to discuss that issue here.

Polishing your shoes and storing them in shoe trees (preferably cedar) is the best way to care for shoes.

Polishing

While there are a myriad of ways to polish shoes, we suggest the following as being one of the simplest methods:

1. Leave the shoe trees in the shoes.

2. Wipe off all dust, dirt, mud, etc. with a clean cloth.

3. Match polish (cream or wax) to color of shoes.

4. Apply polish to shoe with applicator brush. (If you're a seasoned veteran, you may wish to apply a matching ink around the side edge of the soles.)

5. Rub polish into shoe with soft cloth until entire shoe is covered.

6. Lightly brush the shoe with a horsehair polishing brush to bring out the shine. (Don't use too much force.)

7. Briskly buff shoe with soft, *clean* cloth to bring out the luster.

Caution: Polishing shoes can be a messy endeavor. If you have the opportunity, we recommend professional shines. The few dollars it costs will be well worth the money spent.

Because cleaning suedes and other similar types of leathers is a different process, for peace of mind, just take them to a pro.

Shoe Trees

The importance of shoe trees cannot be overemphasized. By the end of the day, the statistical average is that you will produce nearly a half-pint of perspiration. Much of it finds its way into your shoes. Shoe trees not only maintain the form of your shoes, but also serve the added function of drawing the moisture out of the leather, thus allowing your shoes to dry.

Now that the entire business casual wardrobe is in place, a question many men ask is, "Can the clothes I wear mask some of my physical attributes I'd rather not have?" The answer is yes, and in the next chapter we will discuss how.

11

WHEN YOU HAVE SOMETHING TO HIDE

Observe your enemies lest they first find
out your faults.
ANTISTHENES

Average weight for a man

In 1980–173 pounds.
In 1996–180 pounds.

U ntil now we've talked about what a business casual attire can add to your life. In a way, though, it can take away a few things. While your wardrobe can do nothing about your shape or age, by selecting the right casual clothes you can *appear* to be younger, older, or thinner. As always, however, the opposite is also true. By making the wrong choice you can draw attention to your weight or age, worsening the situation you were self-conscious about in the first place. So how do you figure out how to help your figure with a casual wardrobe?

Just Look at Yourself!

Start with a trip to the mirror. Take a look at yourself. You start with a look in the mirror because you have to be honest with yourself.

Now, if in looking in the mirror, you see that you're losing your hair, you'll have to consult another book. But if you see anything from the neck down you're not happy about, we can help with some casual dressing tips.

First, you are always more comfortable in clothing that fits, and the truth is that you look better, too. Too many men cram themselves into a size too small rather than admit that their bodies aren't what they used to be. Don't let your ego get in the way of your good sense. If your pants feel too tight when you sit down, then it's probably time to move up *two* more sizes. Really! If you buy your clothes in the sizes you wore back in college, you may feel nostalgic, but other people know only what they see, which may be your belly hanging over your belt.

Speaking of bellies, that's how it is for most men. Nine times out of ten, when a man gains weight, it's right there around his waist— "the front porch." Let's say you take a vow to work out every day until that gut is gone. As admirable as that is, any man over 30 knows how long it can take to slim down. In the meantime, you can use your wardrobe to mask your middle-age spread. Jackie Gleason, you may recall, was a large man, but he always looked elegant in his clothes.

Buy Your Right Size

Buy whatever size actually fits you, and remember that the same size is cut differently by various clothing companies. So there's no substitute for actually trying the clothes on. Men, though, seem to have a gene that makes trying on clothes unnecessary and troublesome to them. Why should we go into the fitting room? I know my sizes and I can read labels. So shopping for clothes should be as easy as picking up a magazine. Right?

Wrong. Any item of clothing that is sold unwrapped should be tried on before purchase. It's a pain. It's time-consuming. But consider how much more time it'll take when you get home and find out that the size 34 pants you bought actually fit like a size 32 and you have to return them. You could wear those pants holding your breath in, but that gets uncomfortable after a few minutes.

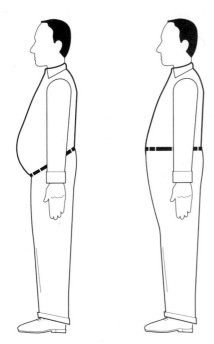

In any case, tight clothing is often more than uncomfortable. While you might think a tight fit looks sexy (it usually has the opposite effect), it's also usually less elegant and less

Wear your pants a little higher

professional. If you have a belly, it is better to buy pants that rise up a little higher at the waist than a little lower, so that your stomach doesn't hang over your belt. Try on different styles until you find one that works. You'll appreciate the extra room. So will your associates who see you. The cardinal rule is not to buy clothes that are too small.

Some Tips on Camouflage

You can also mask love handles from the waist up. Try layering with, say, a T-shirt and a vest, or try a cardigan, something big enough to come down and cover your midsection. Jackets can do the same thing (as long as they're not too short, and they're big enough; see below). In knit shirts and sweaters, try buying up one size to give yourself a little extra room for concealment and comfort. The extra size helps.

Colors can also help your appearance. Generally, lighter colors seem to add pounds to people's looks. Darker colors are usually better for those who are concerned about their weight. Black or navy is the chosen color of many who are very overweight.

Other Tips for the Front Porch

Here are a few other tips for how fashion might help hide what you have:

✔ Don't wear anything tight across your belly, like a sweater. Make sure the rib bottom fits below your stomach. If not, the sweater is too short for you.

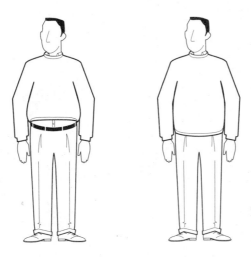

✔ Don't "cut yourself off" at the waist: There should be no major change in colors or patterns from the shirt to the pants, something that immediately draws attention to your waist.

✔ Don't wear horizontal stripes. They just make you look wider. The eye follows the direction of stripes. A heavy-set man wants vertical stripes. The good news is that vertical stripes are at the forefront of today's fashion—in woven shirts and knit polo shirts.

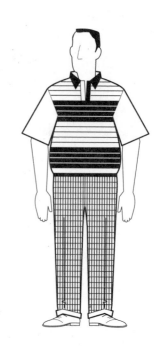

✔ Big checks and plaids and big lapels have the same effect as horizontal stripes. They spread you out. A larger man should avoid these as well.

✔ No short coats. These are just like sawing yourself off in the middle with color changes from top to bottom. You want continuity in color and in pattern, and you want a jacket or sweater long enough to sweep the eye right across the middle, not allow it to linger on your waist.

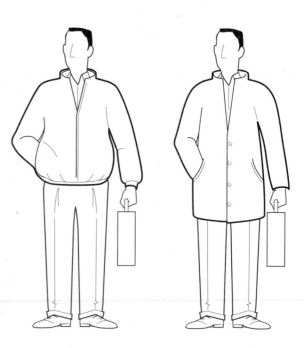

Other Things?

Now a beer belly isn't the only body shape you might want fashion help with.

If you're on the small side, remember our rules about color. Dark colors, which project power and authority, balance out your actual size. You can also add a splash of color in your accessories, like the choice of a tie. A short man might also wear vertical stripes, if they are subtle.

A large man (not overweight, just large-framed), on the other hand, should move toward lighter colors—light gray, heather, tan. Your image is already solid and, if anything, you want to take the edge off a bit by lightening up your palette. As always, with stripes and patterns, the eye follows the line. So a tall or thin man doesn't want vertical stripes that elongate him even more.

If you're concerned about how old you look, the single biggest change you can make is with your hair—whether you have it and what color it is. When it comes to your clothes, business casual wear actually breaks down some of the traditional lines between young and old. In casual wear, no one style of dress is reserved for the older or more established executive. You can wear pretty much anything you look good in. The standard look for one New York executive in the fashion business, a man in his fifties, is simply jeans and a polo shirt. Unless you start dipping into the youth fashions of the day— no earrings, no ponytails, no plastic pants—you don't have to

worry about looking inappropriately young. It's OK to age with grace. You're only as old as you make yourself look.

For young men, it's pretty much the same story. Whether you go for a more contemporary suit, blazer and khakis, or a sweater and jeans, you don't have to be concerned that you'll be seen as dressing beyond your years. If you happen to be very young, or if you look younger than you are, consider moving to the more conservative end of the fashion spectrum at your company and moving to darker colors as a way of giving yourself a little more authority, but that's a matter of degree. You shouldn't look like you've put on your father's clothes to play dress-up, and you don't have to.

But in the end, you must consider this: Unfortunately, how you look is not a "no brainer." You have to bring something to the table. You must understand how you look in what you wear. You and you alone are responsible for understanding how you look best. So open your eyes, gaze into the mirror, and be honest with yourself. And remember to ask yourself this important question: Do your clothes themselves look as good as they can? Are they clean, pressed, and properly tailored? Making your clothes look their best is the subject of the next chapter.

12

MAKING YOUR CLOTHES LOOK THEIR BEST

Again last night I dreamed the dream
called laundry.

JAMES INGRAM MERRILL

You're at a meeting with your supervisor trying to convince her that your ideas have merit and that you're the right person for this project. As you're giving your big pitch you notice that her eyes keep darting down to your shirt. Again and again, she is distracted by something.

After the meeting (which didn't turn out as you'd hoped), you look in the mirror to ask yourself a few questions, and you notice an accessory that you hadn't been aware of: There on your shirt, right between your knit tie and corduroy jacket, is a bright red ketchup stain. What pitch could possibly compete with that?

50% or more (of those surveyed) agree:

I don't like to shop for clothes (53%).

You can't get superior quality unless you're willing to spend more (54%).

Even if you are dressing casually, neatness counts. Let's face it, men aren't known for their laundering and ironing skills. Even though much business casual wear is low-maintenance, every man should know certain basics of how to care for clothing.

Now that you've bought all your casual clothes, you have the right combinations, and you like the way they make you feel, let's discuss how to take care of them. Too often we think that comfortable, casual clothes require less upkeep than expensive suits. This is true to an extent. You could probably get away with throwing a pair of khakis over the back of a chair versus doing the same with a silk shirt. Still, all clothes need to be cared for to look their best. Consider this chapter a survival guide.

A Pop Quiz on Clothing Care

Before we get to the survival information, take the following pop quiz to see how much you know about caring for your clothing. (Don't worry, it's ungraded.)

1. The sleeves of your sport coat should extend

    a. beyond your wrist.

    b. no lower than the bottom of your wrist.

    c. halfway between your wrist and the first bone of your thumb.

2. Shirts put into a washing machine

    a. should have their buttons buttoned.

    b. should never have their buttons buttoned.

    c. should have only the top button buttoned.

3. Turning a garment inside out in the wash will

    a. ruin it.

    b. protect its surface material.

    c. have no effect.

4. When ironing

    a. iron with the grain of the material.

    b. iron against the grain of the material.

    c. This is a trick question. Material has no grain.

5. If a garment is sheer enough to see through,

    a. have it dry cleaned.

    b. wash it in hot water only.

    c. don't ever wash it.

6. When packing clothes for a trip,

    a. keep belts on pants for convenience.

    b. separate belts from pants.

    c. never travel with a belt.

7. When eating a meal while wearing a tie, you should,

    a. never order soup.

    b. tuck the tie into your shirt.

    c. try the veal.

You'll find the answers within the following pages. (You didn't think we'd just give them to you, did you?)

Tailoring

Ask five tailors the same question, and you'll get five different answers. Again, like many aspects of the fashion world, there are no black-and-white rules, no definitively right and wrong answers. However, there are some solid guidelines.

Sport Coats

Sport coats should lie flat and smooth across your shoulders without buckles or creases, while the lapels should neatly hug your chest. If the jacket doesn't fit nicely in the shoulders right off the rack, do not rely on a tailor to make shoulders larger; try a larger size or a different cut. Collars should be smooth around your neck. Do not compromise when it comes to collars. Nothing can ruin the clean lines of a sport coat like a poor fitting collar. The sleeves of the coat should extend no lower than the bottom of your wrist, and the length should hang just far enough to cover the curvature of your rear end.

Pants

A common question asked of most tailors is how long pants should be. When Abraham Lincoln was once asked how long a man's legs should be, according to fashion guru Alan Flusser, Lincoln is said to have quipped, "Long enough to reach the ground." This thought similarly holds true with respect to pants: Pants should be long enough to reach your shoes. Although this may seem patently obvious, you must be careful when it comes to length. If you have too big a break on your shoes, your pants will not only look sloppy, but will also make your legs look shorter. Too small a break and the opposite will hold true. When in doubt, err on the long side. Remember this "fashion introduction" offered by Mr. Flusser, "Shoes, I would like you to meet pants," and you'll never go wrong.

Laundry

Doing your laundry is not an impossible task, but it might as well be judging from the results some men get. While quality clothes (suits and some fabrics) need to be dry cleaned, most casual clothes (shirts, khakis, jeans, socks) can be cleaned in a normal washing machine. But you need to follow some basic rules when doing a load of any size.

Read the Label

First look at the label. All garments come with a care label. This is mandated by the federal government to protect you, the consumer. This is true of an expensive pair of slacks and the T-shirt you bought at the stadium. The label gives you the makeup of the fabric (such as 100% cotton; 70% rayon, 30% cotton; etc.) and basic washing instructions (such as water temperatures, whether to use bleach, how to dry, etc.). If the garment was made overseas (as many casual clothes are), there may be international label symbols. For instance, an iron with an "x" through it means "don't iron." This isn't rocket science, this is done for apparel that will be shipped to different countries.

Wash Before You Wear

Another basic rule in doing laundry is to wash anything you buy before you wear it. The main reason is hygiene: You don't know where that shirt's been or who's tried it on before you. Also, many colored items are full of dyes. If you wear them and they press against your body heat and sweat, the results could be embarrassing. (We're reminded of one young executive who was caught in a sudden downpour wearing a newly bought red shirt. The outcome was not pretty.) Because new clothes tend to "bleed," it's always a good idea to wash them separately the first time.

Separate the Wash

This leads us to another very basic but often overlooked laundry rule (overlooked, anyway, by most men in this country). Colors need to be separated from whites. Anyone who has made the mistake of washing a blue shirt with a load of socks and underwear or adding bleach to a mixed batch of clothes can attest to the fact that it's worth it to take a few extra minutes to create two piles and do two separate loads. Once a piece of clothing is washed enough times, it won't bleed anymore, but why take the chance? (One helpful fact is that black, dark blue, red, and green are the colors that run or bleed the longest.) While many of the clothes we've talked about in this book are not as expensive as suits, your wardrobe expenses will climb needlessly if you have to continually and unnecessarily replace your shirts and pants.

Washday Tips

The water temperature is also important to caring for your clothes. Again, consult the label, but basically, the heavier the fabric is, the hotter the water it can take. Also, the dirtier the item is, the hotter the water it needs.

Follow the label in terms of what detergent to use and whether to use bleach.

Some additional hints include:

✔ Don't overload washing machines. An overloaded machine doesn't clean clothes as thoroughly as possible, and often leads to unbalancing the machine (which stops most washers).

✔ If you're not sure about whether a piece of clothing will be damaged in the wash, turn it inside out. This protects the surface fabric while still cleaning it.

✔ Before washing shirts or pants, button all the buttons and zip all the zippers. This helps the garments keep their shape and prevents snagging and tearing.

✔ Clean out the pockets of any pants or shirts. Items such as ballpoint pens, car keys, tissues, and candy bars aren't really made to go through the spin cycle.

Another valuable piece of information included on the label is the temperature at which a piece of clothing should be dried. (Sometimes it even tells you to line dry it.) Some basic times are:

✔ *Most synthetic fabrics:* 20 minutes on low

✔ *Cottons:* 30–45 minutes on regular (depending on the heaviness)

✔ *Linens:* 15–25 minutes on permanent press

· Look for the cool water instructions!

How you dry clothing and how much you dry it determines whether you should iron it. While the rumpled look may work for college professors, "casual" doesn't mean "wrinkled" in most businesses.

Ironing

Ironing is a necessary evil of caring for your clothes, and isn't really good for your garments. In fact, they'd last a lot longer if you never ironed them. On the other hand, you're not going to close many sales if the surface of your clothes resembles dried fruit. So you need to keep ironing and pressing your clothes, even though it ages them and wears them out. Because of this, you should always use the coolest possible setting on your iron that does the job adequately. Less is often better when it comes to ironing.

Of course, the easiest way to iron is to send out your laundry. This, however, isn't cost-effective with many casual clothes fabrics that are basic, sturdy, and easily ironed at home. So for those of you who think "iron" is a four-letter word, the most basic and important tip is this: Follow any instructions on the label.

Here are some other good tips:

✔ Be sure the iron is always moving. Wiggle it so it doesn't sit on one spot for too long. Burn marks on clothes haven't ever been fashionable.

✔ Don't lean on the iron or put extra pressure on it. The weight of the iron itself should be enough to do the job.

✔ In a pinch, iron only the visible parts of the garment. For example, if you plan on wearing a sweater all day over your shirt, why iron something that is never seen? You only have to iron the collar and the cuffs. (This can be risky, however, because you may want to take off the sweater for many reasons.)

✔ Iron clothes while they are still a little damp. This might mean taking them out of the drier or off the line early. Some people even put their laundry in the refrigerator to keep it damp if they have a large load.

✔ Never iron a shirt that is still wet with perspiration. This stains the shirt forever.

✔ Avoid ironing over buttons and zippers. This can damage both the garment and the iron, let alone break the buttons.

✔ Hang clothes as soon as you take them off. If the day wasn't so rough, you might be able to get by without ironing before the next time you wear the item.

✔ If something isn't badly wrinkled, try hanging it next to a hot shower or using a plant mister or a steamer.

✔ Wash and hang whenever possible. Maytag won't mind, and neither will your clothes.

✔ When packing, try rolling clothes instead of folding them. (See the section on traveling.)

✔ Be careful of the iron's cord. You don't ever want to iron over it or get tangled in it.

✔ Use a sleeveboard for oddly shaped items.

✔ If you're not sure about how a garment will react, experiment on a hidden area. Stop ironing if there are any problems.

✔ Iron with the grain of a material.

One last word on ironing: If you can afford it, send it the laundry or dry cleaner—they know best.

Getting around the Need to Iron

You sometimes need to wear a cleanly pressed shirt for an event after work, and keeping an iron in the office may

not be an option. You can do a few things to cheat and avoid the need to iron. One is to keep an extra shirt at the office. This way, you'll look freshly pressed at the end of the day if you have plans after work. Also, if you're in a position of waiting to go to a meeting or presentation and have some privacy, try not putting on your pants until the last moment. This sounds odd, but you wrinkle pants mainly by sitting in them. If you can wait until the last minute to put them on, you'll at least impress your audience with a fresh look.

One other trick, which works well in negotiations, is often employed by television newscasters. If you pull down on the back bottom of your jacket as you sit down you'll give the impression that your suit is freshly pressed (and impeccably tailored). In other words, it won't bunch up at the collar. We all know how personal appearances can help your position at the bargaining table.

Dry Cleaning

At one time, you knew you were a professional when you knew the person who ran the dry cleaners by his or her first name. Many businessmen swear by their dry cleaners, and it seems that having one is just as important as having a regular dentist or a favorite restaurant. Actually, it is important to have someone you can trust to clean your clothes effectively and efficiently. If no one can recommend a good dry cleaner, ask the Neighborhood Cleaners Association (NCA). This is a

national organization that oversees dry cleaners. While many casual business clothes are machine-washable, many (especially jackets and special fibers) need to be dry cleaned.

What is dry cleaning? Without getting into a long chemistry lesson, dry cleaning is the use of a chemical solvent (usually used to treat stains) and steam to clean clothes with a minimum of water. (Most reputable dry cleaners offer tailoring and mending as well.)

The more practical question is *why* have something dry cleaned? The main reason is because the label tells you to. Be aware, however, that some garments that are labeled as "Dry Clean Only" can probably withstand a machine washing. The manufacturers include the dry cleaning advice on the label as the safest method of cleaning, both to minimize the danger of harming the garment and so that in the long run you will be satisfied with their product.

Other reasons to use dry cleaning include:

✔ If the piece of clothing is tailored. Dry cleaning preserves the construction of the jacket or pant. Some wool garments are contoured by the initial pressing, and only a professional cleaning and pressing keep that same shape. Very often, structured clothing has a special lining that provides ease of movement but that can be damaged by water. Dry cleaning is required.

✔ If there is an unusually large or deep stain.

✔ If there are dyes that will run when wet.

✔ If the garment is sheer. This means the fabric is too delicate to withstand regular washing.

✔ If there is no label and you're simply not sure how to clean it.

Dry Cleaning Mishaps

Dry cleaning is not foolproof. If the dry cleaner misses a spot and doesn't pretreat it, the stain could be made permanent. One example of this is a white wine stain. This is sometimes an invisible stain, but because wine contains acid and sugar, the heat of steaming and pressing makes the stain visible. This is also true of perspiration stains.

While some people think that dry cleaning won't shrink clothes, they're only partially correct. Shrinking occurs; it's just more gradual.

Here are a few tips to guard against dry cleaning mishaps:

✔ Inspect your zippers and buttons to be sure they are in working order and sewn on properly. Remember, orderliness and cleanliness are essential.

✔ Inspect your clothes before you take them to the cleaners so that you know whether a stain wasn't removed or a new stain has appeared.

✔ Point out to your dry cleaner any stains that need pretreatment.

✔ Inspect your clothes when picking them up. Look them over before leaving the store so that you know the job was done correctly and so that any problems can be addressed immediately.

✔ Make sure your instructions to the cleaner are clear. Communication is one of the main problems in business, and, since this is a business transaction, there should be no confusion about what you expect.

✔ Have any rips or tears repaired before dry cleaning.

How Often to Dry Clean

Finally, how often should you have clothes dry cleaned? There's no set answer to this question. Generally you can tell when something is dirty or wrinkled. Clothes made of silk or wool can be worn several times between cleanings. Often, all you have to do is air them out or run a warm iron over them. Synthetic materials, however, probably need to be cleaned more often.

Dry cleaning something too often can result in damage to the clothing. For example, wools and cashmere can be harmed if they are dry cleaned too often. Frequent dry cleaning makes white cottons and linens turn gray. On the other hand, remember that even casual clothes have a limited life. Most jackets and sweaters have a life span of five to ten years.

Constant wearing and cleaning take their toll. Even leather coats, while expected to last a lifetime, are vulnerable to atmospheric conditions, your body, and normal wear and tear.

Travel

A lot of problems can be avoided when clothes are packed correctly for traveling. Since travel is a part of many businessmen's lives, you should know some things about how to keep your clothes looking good while on the road. While it's easy to travel with casual clothes, you should still take precautions so that you don't look too casual. Wrinkles are not an acceptable accessory.

Usually it's a good idea to travel with two bags. One can be a soft bag for carrying small items and flat clothes that can be rolled instead of folded. The other should be a garment bag for hanging jackets and pants. (It's also a good idea to clean your bags from time to time, since they collect oil or dirt from baggage bins on planes and cabs.) Try at all times to carry your bags on the plane. The airlines that were notorious for losing bags are getting worse. We're tempted to name names.

A common problem is how the clothes are packed and in what order. If you're using a suitcase, pack pants on the bottom. Jackets and coats should go in next. These should be followed by shoes, which should be placed in the corners that will be on the bottom when the suitcase is closed. Then pack any knit sweaters, underwear, and socks. Then come the ties. The top layer should be reserved for shirts.

Here are a few other travel tips:

✔ Empty the pockets and remove belts when packing pants.

✔ When hanging pants, make sure the bar is about 10 inches below the waist, then fold the legs over the bar below the knees.

✔ Always use plastic between garments. It will preserve creases.

✔ Center a hanger when hanging a jacket. Turn up the collar.

✔ Don't button jackets. Button the middle button on shirts.

✔ Stack ties together, unless they're silk.

Storage

Traveling isn't the only time that you need to hang and pack your clothes so that they don't get wrinkled and worn. The same thing can happen at home. Here are a few suggestions when storing your casual clothes:

✔ Air out your clothes before putting them into confined spaces, such as drawers and closets. This allows any residual perspiration to dry out.

✔ Button the top button on your shirts when putting them on hangers. This makes the shirt hang straighter and results in fewer wrinkles. If you have the time, button the bottom button as well.

✔ Keep the door on closets open from time to time. Otherwise they tend to smell musty.

✔ Don't cram too much into one drawer. There's no prize for seeing how many shirts you can get into a limited space. The lighter the shirt goes in, the fresher it looks coming out.

✔ As already mentioned, ties can be rolled rather than hung. When you do this, start with the narrow end.

✔ Twice a year, clean out all your drawers and wipe the inside surface with a damp cloth or sponge.

Wearing casual clothes doesn't mean giving them any less care when putting them away at the end of the day.

Stains

Remember that casual wear is only acceptable if it is clean. This book is not a homemaking guide, but businessmen often encounter stains when they're at work or on the road. They sometimes get spots on their shirts or pants during lunch, or they notice stains on their ties as they're getting off the plane on the way to an important meeting. Or they drop pens on their khakis, leaving an ugly ink blot. Eating habits aside, as you wear lighter colors more often, you may start noticing such stains more frequently.

So here are a few tips for the traveling businessman—or even just the sloppy businessman:

✔ Try not to lay your briefcase flat on the floor or ground. It rubs or bounces against you as you walk, dirtying your pants. At least keep all luggage items clean.

✔ If you don't wear an undershirt, be sure to let your deodorant dry completely before you put on your regular shirt. Ironically, the substance you use to prevent sweating often stains worse than the perspiration.

✔ If you're going to be doing something at work that might be messy (such as changing ink or toner), wear something protective, like an apron or an old shirt.

✔ Tuck your tie into your shirt or flip it over your shoulder when eating. Crackers are the only thing that should be dunked in your soup.

✔ If you spill something on yourself during a meal, get to it immediately. Scrape off as much as you can and then blot the stain with a wet napkin. It's also a good idea to place a second, dry napkin between the fabric and your skin. Cold water is usually best, but club soda often does the trick as well. Try not to rub a stain too hard; pat it as much as you can. But in general, if you stain a tie, forget it. It's too late. Soup and gravy, after all, is the lifeline of the neckware industry!

✔ When traveling, take along a small vial of detergent for emergencies.

It's impossible to go through life stain-free. But how you deal with stains can often make the difference between keeping a garment and having to replace it.

13

CREATING A CASUAL DRESS POLICY FOR YOUR COMPANY

Birds of a feather will gather together.
SIR RICHARD BURTON

Keep up appearances whatever you do.
CHARLES DICKENS

50% or more (of those surveyed) agree:

Can wear casual clothes to work (70%).

Normally do not wear a jacket to work (63%).

N ow you know all about how to create a casual wardrobe for yourself. What about creating a casual dress policy for your workplace—keeping in mind that your business is still a business?

In general, going business casual can have *real* benefits. For example, it can help break down internal barriers between management and associates, between the suits and the production workers, between white collars and blue, and even between younger and older workers. Another benefit is to empower associates, to give them the opportunity to be comfortable on the job, to give them an opportunity to dress in a way that reflects more of who they are and to imply that they're trusted to do the right thing with that freedom. Going business casual generally doesn't require an explicit dress code. In fact, sometimes spelling it out can have the opposite effect. An explicit written dress code can transform all the benefits into simply another regulation from top management—giving a measure of freedom with one hand, and taking it back with the other by spelling out exactly how to exercise that freedom.

That said, however, you can still express preferences to your associates about business casual wear. You may even find that in a more traditional office, where the move to business casual is a big one, associates *want* some specific guidelines about what to wear and not wear.

Where to Begin?

The starting point for any workplace casual dress code is that the focus needs to be on business, its culture, and its work, not on the fashion. What works for company A might not work for company B. There are many different types of companies and corporate cultures. Different types of work are done at various offices. Also, in larger companies, different departments have different needs and requirements. Only you know your company best. So you need to consider all these aspects when starting to think about a casual dress code.

Business casual wear doesn't have to detract from the job; in fact, it should be presented to everyone as another tool for getting the job done. Once each person understands that he or she is always representing the company—no matter what the new policy on dressing for work might become—business casual wear can help present a modern, focused, friendly image to customers. If your own top management still isn't sure, you might point to the experience of any number of the previously mentioned major companies that have gone casual and prospered. Of course, if a meeting outside the office calls for a suit and tie, that obligation takes precedence over any formal or informal dress code.

The actual mix of casual items in your office depends on the work you do, the comfort level of your associates (and of top management), and the nature of your contacts with people outside the company. Business casual wear that is appropriate for a small ad shop is probably not appropriate in a large corporate law firm. By now you should have a good sense of the range that works in either setting. Also, your associates have a pretty good sense as well. Anecdotally, at least, the evidence says that most companies find their associates make the right decisions about what will work fashionwise in their office.

While a detailed dress code may not be a good idea, feel free, if associates seem to want it, to suggest a range of do's and don'ts: for example, no T-shirts, no sweatshirts with slo-

gans or pictures, or no shorts. Many say no jeans. We disagree, but it is your company. Create a list of what you'd want to see your associates wear (Izod shirts, for example) and what you wouldn't (such as sandals). If you're visually inclined, you can even put together a portfolio of acceptable looks, drawn from magazines, fashion sections, and other sources. Many clothing manufacturers also offer information in print or on video about business casual wear.

If your company has no casual dress policy, you might find that your associates are ready to go from zero to sixty and go casual five days a week right away. You might want to ease into the policy, beginning with one day a week or for special occasions. Whenever you step on the pedal, make sure you know where you want to go.

Finally, here are a few general guidelines:

✔ Associates who are uncomfortable dressing casually should be encouraged to wear what they find comfortable (a suit, for example). The point of business casual is not to estrange anyone, customer or associate. Sooner or later, they will join in.

✔ Start by putting together a team of people from a cross section of the company. They in turn should create a policy for "corporate appropriateness."

✔ Whatever an associate wears should be clean, neat, and in good repair.

✔ Clothing that looks as though it would be more at home in another setting, such as the beach or the backyard, probably belongs there.

It might seem like a big change for a company in which business dress has been traditional, but, almost without exception, companies that have moved to casual business dress have been pleased with the results, and that goes from the CEO all the way down the line.

Whether it's a boost in associate morale, a rise in productivity, or a perk to attract prospective associates, business casual wear works.

Nevertheless, it is equally important that someone be able to tell associates when they are dressed inappropriately. The human resources department is usually best equipped for this task.

We've included some sample dress codes in Appendix B of the book to give you an idea of specifically how a few companies went about spelling out (or not spelling out) the do's and don'ts. You'll also find a general guide for creating a casual dress policy announcement.

Conclusion

Take nothing on its looks; take everything on
evidence. There's no better rule.

CHARLES DICKENS, *Great Expectations*

We hope you now have a better idea how to dress casually for success. You should be able to go out on your own, purchase, coordinate, and maintain everything you need for a business casual wardrobe.

While it's okay to use the lists and quizzes in this book as reference points, by now you will have taken that information and started to formulate your own personal approach to dressing casually in the workplace. Your clothes should always reflect the true you.

How you dress is part of who you are. Since no one can tell you who to be, no one can tell you which clothes are right for you, casual or formal. The decisions should be only yours.

So get to work. Roll up your sleeves. And don't be afraid to leave them that way. We are at the ***end of the beginning*** of casual dressing for success. Good luck, enjoy, and thanks for reading.

A

CREATING A COMPANY CASUAL DRESS POLICY ANNOUNCEMENT

As with any written policy, be as concise as possible. The policy should have three parts:

Part 1. Announce that you've decided to initiate a casual dress policy, and explain why you're doing so. Make sure your associates know what you hope to accomplish with the policy. What is your definition of "casual"? Be brief but clear. Establish a team with goals, directives, timetables for implementation, and approval by senior management.

Part 2. Which clothing items are appropriate? Identify clothing categories (pants, shirts, shoes, etc.) and give examples of acceptable casual wear for each.

There's no need to explain *why* items are acceptable. Just identify them.

Part 3. Which clothing items are not appropriate? List them in the same format as in Part 2. Be as specific as possible. Mention that the employees should also use their common sense when deciding whether an item is appropriate for the office.

Tell them to check with a manager if they're not sure about an item.

B

SAMPLE BUSINESS CASUAL POLICIES

PHILLIPS-VAN HEUSEN CORPORATION

1290 AVENUE OF THE AMERICAS NEW YORK N Y 10104 (212) 541-5200

TO: NYO Associates

FROM: Personnel

DATE: Jan. 20, 1994

Re: Wardrobe Guidelines

Phillips-Van Heusen is committed to creating a professional workplace environment. Many factors contribute to a professional image, one of which is proper business attire.

To assist in discerning between business and casual attire a wardrobe guideline has been established which should be followed at all times.

The following is a list of unacceptable and acceptable business attire. This list does not constitute a comprehensive listing but rather a guideline to provide the associate with a general idea of proper business attire:

Unacceptable Work Attire Mon.-Fri.	Acceptable Work Attire Fri. only
Sweatpants/sweatshirts Jogging suits	Jeans (no rips/cuts/holes) Collared shirts (banded/ turtleneck acceptable)

Leggings
Sneakers, thongs, sandals
Strapless tops/dresses,
  tank tops, halter tops
  (unless worn with
  jacket or cardigan)
	Tie optional
	Sweaters
	Any Mon.-Thurs. attire

Dress casually on Fridays but keep in mind that this is a professional workplace. If you are in doubt as to whether or not to wear something, it probably is inappropriate. "When in doubt—don't."

PHILLIPS-VAN HEUSEN CORPORATION
CENTRAL OFFICE
BRIDGEWATER, NEW JERSEY

PERSONNEL PRACTICES AND PROCEDURES

TITLE: DRESS CODE COVERAGE: ALL ASSOCIATES

1. <u>GENERAL</u>

   A. Company policy regarding dress codes requires that all associates dress in a business-like manner. As a fashion-oriented business, the Company encourages associates to dress professionally at all times.

   B. It is necessary to distinguish between business and casual clothes. Good judgement should be used when determining suitable office attire.

2. <u>ASSOCIATE GUIDELINES</u>

   A. Following is a list of appropriate and inappropriate business attire. This list does not constitute a comprehensive listing, but rather, guidelines to provide the associate with a general idea of appropriate business attire.

   B. <u>APPROPRIATE ATTIRE</u>
   - dresses (tailored)
   - skirts & blouses
   - dress slacks & blouse
   - suits (business)
   - coordinated accessories
   - suit & tie
   - shirt & tie with dress slacks, coordinating jacket, vest, sweater
   - business shoes
   - socks/stockings
   - corporate shorts (check with your supervisor if you are unsure if your shorts are corporate)

   <u>INAPPROPRIATE ATTIRE</u>
   - denim jeans or skirt (regardless of color)
   - tank or tee tops
   - shorts
   - spandex pants
   - jogging suits
   - short mini skirts
   - strapless tops
   - strapless dresses (except with coordinating jacket)
   - sneakers
   - sandals
   - leggings/cotton or lycra pants
   - sweatpants/sweatshirts

Note: Hosiery must be worn at all times.

PROFESSIONAL DRESS STANDARDS

As a leader in the fashion world, PVH encourages all associates to dress professionally at all times. Company policy regarding dress code requires that all associates dress in a business-like manner. If you have any question as to whether particular attire is appropriate, please see a Human Resource Representative for clarification.

The following is a list of appropriate and inappropriate business attire. This does not constitute a comprehensive listing, but rather, guidelines to provide you a general idea of appropriate business attire at PVH.

APPROPRIATE	INAPPROPRIATE
Dresses	Denim jeans or skirts
Skirts & Blouses	(regardless of color)
Dress slacks	Tank or Tee tops
Business Suits	Spandex
Coordinated Access.	Jogging Suits
Suit and Tie	Sweatshirts or Sweatpants
Shirt & Tie with Dress	Strapless Tops & Dresses
Slacks, coordinating	(except with coordinating
Jacket, Vest, Sweater	jacket)
Business Shoes	Sneakers
Socks/Hosiery	Sandals
Corporate Shorts/Skirts	Shorts (tight fitting and
(loose fitting & slightly	well above the knee)
above the knee)	

HOSIERY MUST BE WORN AT ALL TIMES

The Bridgewater facility has adopted a relaxed dress code on Fridays. Please note, however, that although the dress code is relaxed, certain items of clothing are still considered inappropriate for Friday dress. Listed below are items considered appropriate/inappropriate for Friday. Keep in mind that this is not a comprehensive listing, but rather, guidelines to provide you with a general idea of the relaxed dress code.

APPROPRIATE	INAPPROPRIATE
Collared Shirts	Short mini skirts
(short or long sleeved)	Sneakers
Blouses/Sweaters	Short Shorts
Skirts	T-Shirts
Cotton pants and jeans	Jogging Suits
Corporate Shorts	Sweatshirts, Sweatpants,
Any item included in	leggings, biking shorts
the corporate dress	Open-toe sandals
code policy above.	

FAR EAST DRESS CODE

The goal of the dress code is two-fold:

1) To provide a more enjoyable and comfortable work
   environment hence increase productivity

2) To ensure our operation presents a professional business-
   like manner at all times

For Mondays through Thursdays, with the exception of when we
have visitors from the United States or appointments that
require more formal attire the following guidelines will be
used. Please note that this is not a comprehensive listing,
but rather, guidelines to help you understand the "spirit" of
the dress code.

Appropriate items

Woven collared shirts (short or long sleeved)
Blouses/Sweaters
Skirts
"Dressy" casual slacks
Dress Slacks
"Corporate" shorts (women)
Socks/hosiery
Dresses
Leggings with big shirts
Dress shirts/Ties   ) on days that they
Suits   ) are appropriate

Inappropriate items

Jeans
Sneakers
Short shorts
Jogging suits
Sweatshirts
Biking shorts
Open toe sandals
Strapless tops (except with coordinating jacket)
Tank tops

For Fridays when no U.S. visitors are present in the office:

<u>Appropriate items</u>

Knit collared shirts
Jeans
Sweatshirts
Cotton slacks/casual slacks
<u>plus</u> all appropriate items for Monday through Thursday

<u>Inappropriate items</u>

Sneakers
Short shorts
Jogging suits
Sweatpants
Biking shorts
Strapless tops (except with coordinating jacket)
Open toe sandals

Should our U.S. visitors wish to dress casual during their stay in our office the casual dress code for the day in question would apply. That is Mondays-Thursdays code or Fridays code for the respective days.

One word about dress code enforcement. If we all don't comply with the above codes the privilege will be taken away for all of us. In the event that an associate fails to dress in accordance with this new policy, his/her supervisor may take the following steps:

1) On the first occasion, the offending associate will be given a verbal warning along with a copy of this policy. Documentation regarding the warning will be placed n the associate's personnel file.

2) On the second occasion, the supervisor may ask the offending associate to return home to change into proper attire and then return back to work. The violation will be documented as a written warning and placed in the associate's personnel file.

3) On the third occasion, the supervisor will send the offending associate home without pay, or take more severe action if the violation is flagrant. This violation will be documented and placed in the associate's personnel file

We believe this dress code represents an added benefit to our associates and our operation. As a rule of thumb if you are in doubt as to the appropriateness of clothing to be worn to the office, don't wear it! Check with your supervisor first.

CHEVRON REFINING

Richmond, California
February 23, 1996

No. 27 - RICHMOND DRESS CODE GUIDELINES

The Management Team with cross-functional guidance has determined that a more relaxed dress code is appropriate for our management/administrative work force. The new guidelines can best be described as "informal business attire."

The major change in the new guidelines is that neckties are now optional. However, each employee's business activities and working environment must determine what is suitable business dress on a daily basis. For example, meetings with some customers, visitors to the refinery or attendance at some meetings in the City may prompt the need for traditional business clothing, including a necktie. Employees who work consistently in the refinery should dress appropriately for that work situation.

The appropriate level of "informal business attire" can best be described as: blouses, collared shirts (no T-shirts), slacks including, for example, "Dockers" (no shorts, denim jeans, sweats), street shoes (no athletic shoes, sandals). This policy applies even if Nornex coveralls are worn by individuals from time to time.

We want to continue to represent Chevron in a business-like and professional manner and hope this makes our refinery a more open and comfortable place to work.

This policy change is effective immediately.

W. D. STEELMAN

San Ramon, CA
July 22, 1993

INFORMAL BUSINESS ATTIRE

CCC SAN RAMON EMPLOYEES:

On June 30, the Leadership Team announced "informal business attire" may be worn on any or all work days, as deemed appropriate by location management. Effective immediately, all Chevron Chemical San Ramon employees may wear "informal business attire" every day.

As background, our predominating interest is that all Chevron Chemical employees continue to focus on our Vision, which calls for "dedicated employees with a passion for meeting customer needs" both internal and external. Unlike many other Chevron Opco's which have adopted relaxed dress codes, Chevron Chemical Company is, principally, an externally oriented business. Therefore, guidelines are aimed at providing a more comfortable work environment while also maintaining the kind of business-like image and atmosphere our customers have come to expect.

Following are guidelines on what constitutes appropriate "informal business attire" at Chevron Chemical. The guidelines are based on current practices in various Chevron Chemical Divisions, recent survey information from the Society of Human Resource Management and related literature from other business sources.

INFORMAL BUSINESS ATTIRE GUIDELINES

Along with business suits, ties, dress shoes, or sport coats for men or dresses, blouses, skirts and heel shoes for women, the following will be considered acceptable:

MEN	WOMEN
Dress Slacks	Slacks
Dress shirts w/collars & full buttons in front (no polo or golf)	Split skirts (culottes)
	Pant suits
Semi-dress loafers	Flat shoes/casual (no tennis)
	Knee-length walking shorts w/hose

It is obviously impossible to develop guidelines that are sufficiently descriptive and detailed to cover the full range of clothing options. Ultimately, we are relying on the good judgment and sense of professionalism of individual employees and supervisors.

Thank you for your support and cooperation.

J. E. PEPPERCORN

HELLER FINANCIAL CFG
BUSINESS CASUAL DRESS CODE GUIDELINES

Although Business Casual Days allow for a less formal style of dress, it is still necessary for employees to dress professionally—or in a "business-casual" style.

Although we cannot think of every possible clothing option, the following guidelines should help you determine what type of dress is appropriate for Business Casual Days. Overall, the success of Business Casual Days will depend on the good judgment of all employees.

The following are guidelines for acceptable and unacceptable business-casual dress:

1. Footwear

Generally, any dress or casual shoes are acceptable with the exception of athletic shoes, hiking boots or sandals.

2. Pants

Trousers or slacks, including dress or casual, are acceptable with the exception of jeans (regardless of color or material), sweat pants, stretch pants, stirrup pants or shorts.

3. Dresses/Jumpers/Skirts

Casual dresses, jumpers and skirts, including split skirts (skorts), are acceptable with the exception of sun dresses and denim. Extremely short dresses or skirts are unacceptable.

4. Shirts/Blouses

Short-sleeved and long-sleeved shirts are acceptable, including rugby or "polo" type shirts. Ties are optional.

Sweatshirts, T-shirts, tank tops, halter tops, low cut garments, or extremely tight clothing are *not* acceptable.

5. Sweaters/Jackets/Vests

Generally, anything that coordinates with the rest of the attire is acceptable. Off-the-shoulder styles are *not* acceptable.

6. Hats/Jewelry

Hats or full head coverage (other than for religious purposes) are *not* acceptable. Please accessorize conservatively.

When in doubt, check with your Manager or your Human Resources representative first.

GUIDELINES FOR DRESS AT CLOROX

People still have questions about both regular and casual dress and what is and isn't acceptable wear at Clorox. Based on these questions, HR has prepared these guidelines so that we are all in synch with how to maintain an environment in which we can all be proud to work.

Monday through Thursday

- **Because our business environment today is faster-paced and less formal, dress standards during the week have relaxed a bit.**
  - **Remember that while at work you are always representing Clorox.** Dress appropriately for your day's work. Dress traditionally when others will also be more formal.
  - **Otherwise,** a sport coat/dress slacks combination for men is acceptable; and as always, blazers, slacks and pantsuits are appropriate for women.

Friday

- **You're still representing Clorox.** Casual clothing should make you and everyone you work with comfortable.
- **Friday is the only day** designated as "casual dress day."
  - Exceptions are made during the annual GIFT campaign when you can buy special buttons.
  - For some all-day <u>off-site</u> meetings, casual dress may be acceptable (and if so, it should be communicated in advance to participants).
  - It is not appropriate to be in the company's offices dressed casually, except on Fridays. Take this into consideration even if you may not be in the office a full day.
- Take your day's schedule into account, and **present yourself in a manner appropriate to your environment and your day's work.**
  - Sometimes that means casual dress, sometimes not. If you have a meeting scheduled on a Friday with outside visitors, dress more traditionally if casual dress is inappropriate.
- **Pick clothing that is comfortable yet communicates a professional attitude.**
  - Combine some of your existing business wardrobe with casual attire. For example, try wearing a button-down shirt with khakis and loafers, either with a more colorful tie/scarf or just a sport coat or sweater.
  - Leave your jeans (any color), T-shirts, jogging suits or sweats, and beach/river sandals at home. Wear shirts with collars.
  - Avoid clothing that is too revealing or tight-fitting, including leggings.
- Wear clothing that's clean, pressed or wrinkle-free, and without holes or frayed areas.
  - When in doubt, leave it out.
- **Check with your manager if you have any questions or call the HR Service Center, Ext. 7095. A brochure providing examples of casual dress is also available from the Service Center.**

CLOROX BUSINESS CASUAL

<u>QUESTIONS AND ANSWERS</u>

1) What does "business casual" mean?

A) At all times, employees are expected to dress in a professional manner, recognizing that acceptable personal appearance is a matter of common sense and good taste. As with today's traditional business attire, appropriate "business casual" will be determined over time. As a general rule, "business casual" attire would include slacks, sweaters, skirts, sport shirts, casual shoes, etc. Some clothing, such as shorts, halter tops, sweat clothes, jeans with holes, and tights or leggings, etc. are inappropriate for a professional environment.

2) What do you mean by "dress appropriately for your audience/customer"?

A) In all situations, what you wear should make your audience/customer feel comfortable. If, for example, you are interfacing with customers who continue to dress in a more traditional business manner, you should follow their lead. Likewise, if you are representing IBM at a meeting or a conference where traditional business attire is more appropriate, you would be expected to dress more formally. If in doubt, traditional business standards should continue to be the place to start.

3) Is "business casual" a requirement?

A) No, "business casual" is an OPTION that is available to employees as an alternative to "business formal," if it is appropriate for your audience/customers. Many employees, based on their current wardrobe, or what they may feel comfortable with, may wish to continue to dress in traditional business manner. In all situations, we expect that employees will respect their colleagues' choices whether it be to dress "business formal" or "business casual."

INDEX

ABOUT VAN HEUSEN

In 1881, an enterprising immigrant family began making and selling shirts to coal miners in the Pottsville, Pennsylvania area. The shirts were made well and wore well, and a new company was born. This company grew, investing in capacity, engineering, and, more importantly, its people. Treating people with dignity was the mainstay for the company.

In the late 1940s and early 1950s, two paramount events took place that would set the course for the future of the company. First, a Dutch inventor named Van Heusen developed and patented a revolutionary process for fusing linings to collars. The net effect was the creation of a nonwrinkling collar, an item of apparel that had never before been available. (In fact, today the technology has improved, but the fundamental principle of the engineering feat is still in place.) The company acquired the rights to the patent and then took the second and defining step for the future: The name of the company was changed to the Van Heusen Shirt Company. Seeking to establish Van Heusen as a household name, a national brand-building campaign was then launched. Soon, television programs, stadiums, and billboards featured Van Heusen ads. And celebrity endorsers such as Tony Curtis and Ronald Reagan lined up to be featured pitchmen. Even Andy Warhol immortalized the Van Heusen brand with a rendition of the Ronald Reagan ad.

The 1960s and 1970s were marked by innovative new product introductions and ever-growing market share. In the 1980s, management recognized that in order to continue expanding, the company needed to become involved in outfitting the consumer from head to toe. Accordingly, a plan for the strategic acquisition of top brands in different clothing categories was put in place. To give the company a presence in the footwear business, G. H. Bass Shoe Company was acquired. Today, Bass is the largest casual footwear company in the country. Then, to position Van Heusen in the knitwear and sportswear business, Izod, Izod Club, and Gant were acquired. These acquisitions accelerated Van Heusen to the forefront of the growing sportswear, golf, and corporate casual sportswear business.

Today, Van Heusen is the largest dress shirt, sweater, and casual footwear company in the United States, with annual sales of well over $1 billion, and is leading the effort to casualize the workplace—while retaining its core dress shirt position.

When people think Van Heusen, the think not only quality and durability, but, because our products are worn both for work and for play, they think trust, pride, comfort, and success. Treating people with dignity is still the mainstay for our company.